T0306555

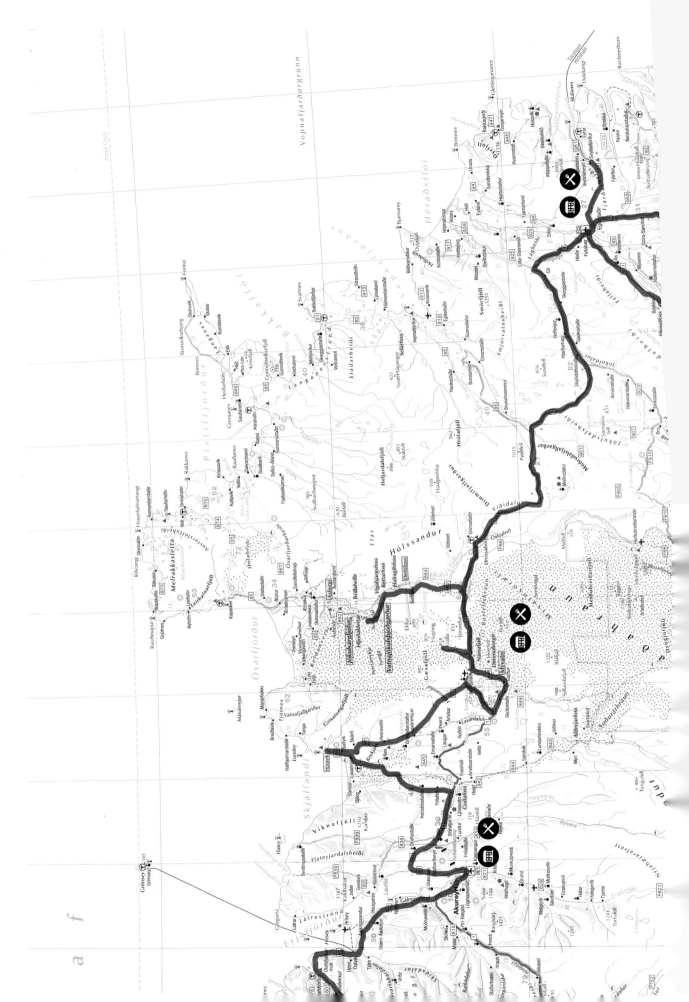

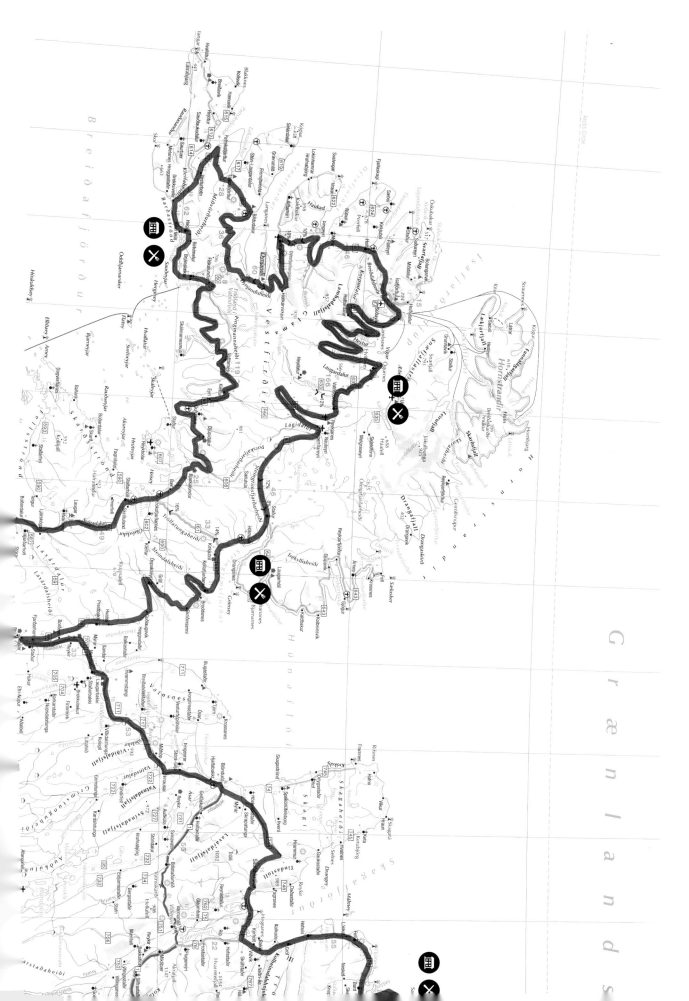

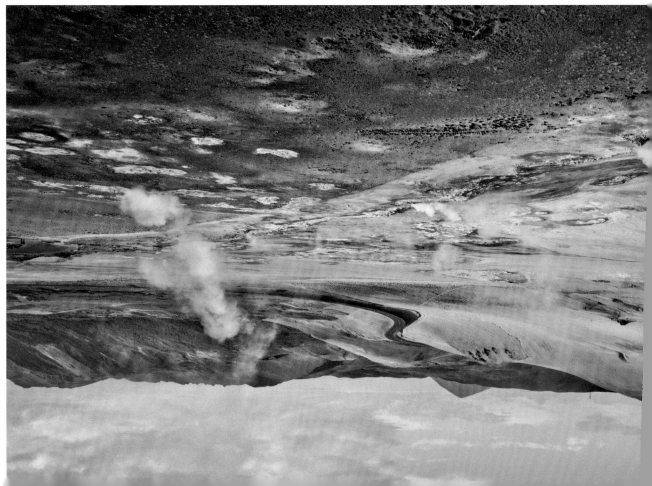

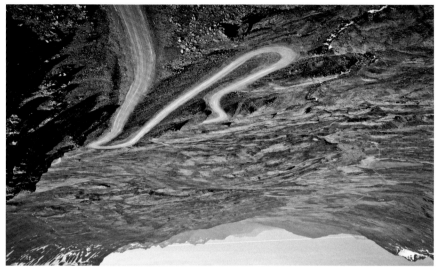

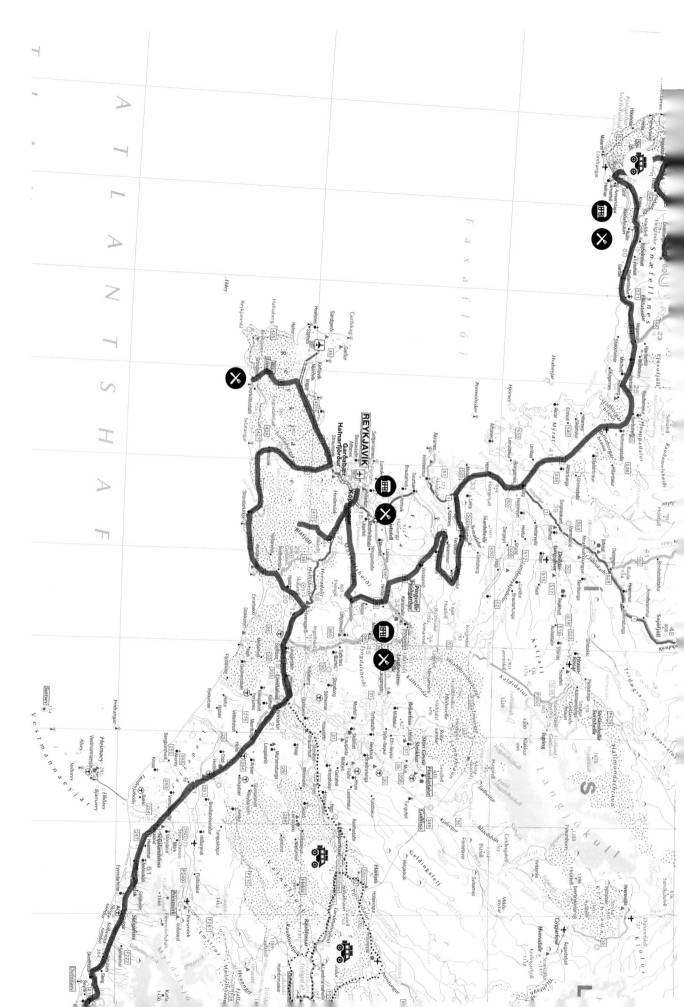

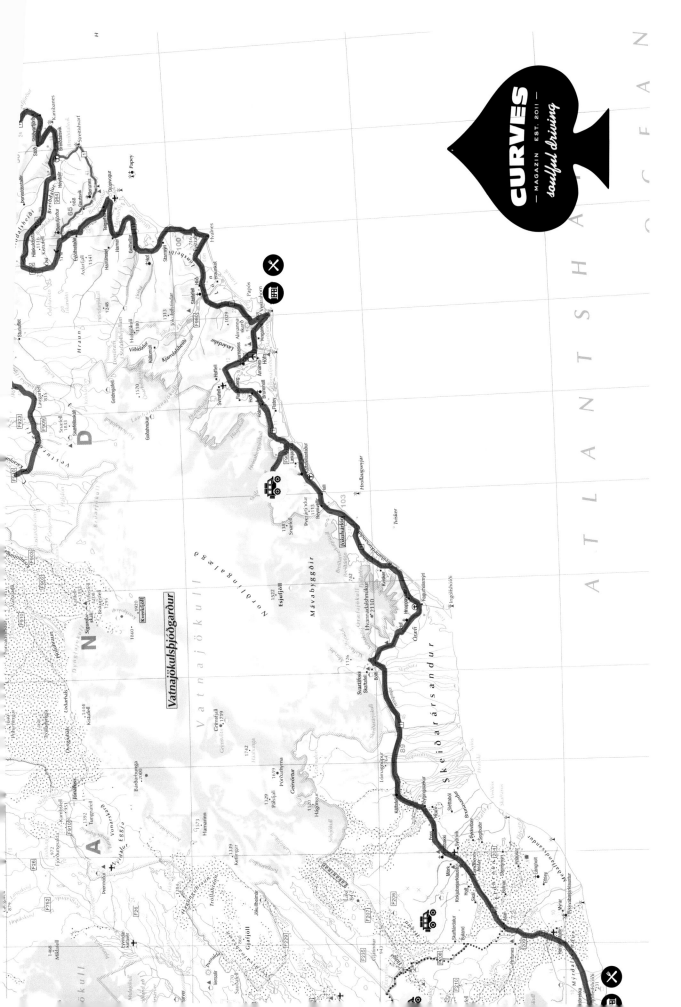

CURVES
— MAGAZIN EST. 2011 —
soulful driving

TAGHEUER.COM

INTRO

Island. Die Vulkaninsel am nördlichen Polarkreis ist ein Sehnsuchtsort, mit großartiger Natur, rauem Wetter und herrlichen Geheimnissen. Genau deshalb passt diese Reise nach Island so ausgezeichnet in die CURVES-Erzählungen: Fernweh und magische Erlebnisse sind neben purer Fahrfreude der eigentliche Antrieb des Unterwegsseins im CURVES-Rhythmus. Und weil die Energie Islands aus Wind, Wasser und dem Feuer der Erde gemacht ist, konnten wir manche Etappen unserer Reise sogar damit bestreiten: Island per Elektroauto, das geht durch die Infrastruktur-Investitionen der unorthodox denkenden Isländer immer besser – mehr dazu auf den „Backstage"-Seiten dieser Ausgabe. Jede Ausgabe dieser Reihe hat ihren ganz eigenen Charakter, aber die Reise nach Island ist mit Sicherheit ein ganz besonderer Höhepunkt: Die schiere Menge an unvergleichlich dramatischen Fotografien, die Geschichten von beklemmenden, wunderbaren, magischen und friedlichen Momenten erzählen, hat uns bei der Gestaltung dieses Bands begeistert. Erleben Sie mit uns ein wahres Feuerwerk von Emotionen entlang Islands großer Kurve: der Ringstraße um die Insel. Hinauf zu den Westfjorden, in den äußersten Osten, zu den Vulkanen im Süden. Fahren Sie mit uns, staunend und ergriffen, offen für jeden Moment dieser einmaligen Reise. Soulful Driving mit CURVES auf Island.

—

Iceland: the volcanic island half-way to Greenland is a place filled with longing, great natural beauty, extreme weather and wonderful secrets. That's exactly why this trip to Iceland makes the perfect fit for the CURVES series: wanderlust and magical experiences, as well as sheer driving pleasure, are what provide the impetus for following the rhythm of the CURVES beat. Because Iceland's energy comes from wind, water and the fire of the earth, we were even able harness these forces to cover some stages of our journey: infrastructural investment by the freethinking Icelanders means that it is getting easier and easier to choose to travel by electric car – you'll find more information in the "Backstage" pages of this issue. Each issue in this series has its own particular character, but the trip to Iceland is certainly a very special highlight: the sheer number of incomparably dramatic photographs tell stories of overpowering, wonderful, magical and tranquil moments, helping us put together this volume. Join us to experience a real firework of emotions along the orbital route that encompasses Iceland. We travel up to the western fjords, to the extreme east and to the volcanoes in the south. Come with us on an amazing and moving journey and open your mind to every moment of this unique trip: soulful driving with CURVES in Iceland.

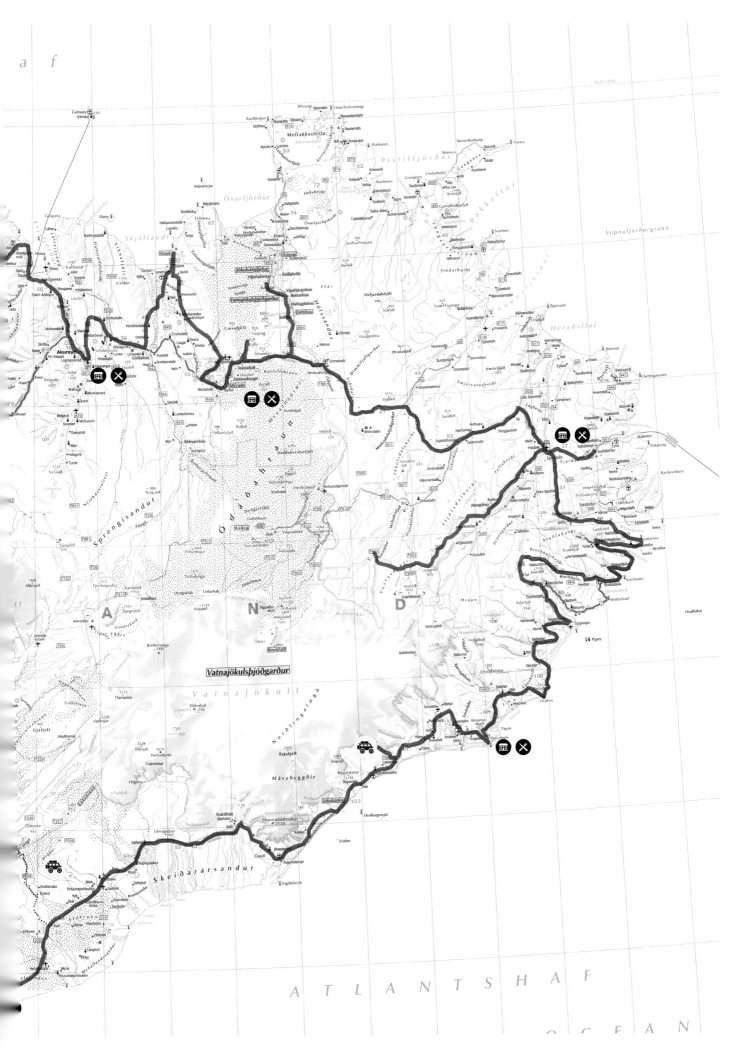

JÖKULSÁRLÓN

1
ETAPPE
STAGE

2
ETAPPE
STAGE

Die Hauptstadt Islands steht am Beginn dieser Reise, nicht nur, weil sie das beinahe einzige internationale Tor auf die Insel ist, sondern weil sie viel über Island erklärt. Die Geschichte, die Moderne, das aufgeschlossene und gleichzeitig eigensinnige Wesen der Isländer. Und man kann sich in Reykjavík akklimatisieren, mit einer kleinen Schonfrist auf die Schroffheit Islands einstellen. Von hier aus fahren wir zuerst ein Stück weit ins Landesinnere, besuchen den Þingvellir-Nationalpark und streben dann an der Westküste Islands entlang nach Norden. Eine Runde über die Halbinsel des Snaefellsjökull muss sein, viele Kilometer später landen wir auf der Halbinsel Vestfirðir, die sich mit ihrer von Fjorden zerfurchten Küstenlinie weit hinaus in die Grönlandsee erstreckt. Wir umrunden die sogenannte Westfjord-Halbinsel und machen uns dann im äußersten Norden Islands auf den Weg zu einer Stadt am Eyjafjörður: Akureyri.

This trip begins in Iceland's capital, not just because it is almost the only international gateway to the island, but also because it tells us a lot about Iceland: its history and modernity, as well as the open-minded and at the same time stubborn nature of the Icelanders. Reykjavík also offers a chance to acclimatize, a short grace period as you adjust to the ruggedness of Iceland. From here we first head inland, visiting the Þingvellir National Park and then taking off to the north along the west coast of Iceland. A circuit of the Snaefellsjökull Peninsula is not to be missed. Many kilometers later we reach the Vestfirðir peninsula, which stretches far out into the Greenland Sea with its fjord-rutted coastline. We circumnavigate the Westfjord Peninsula and then set off for the far north of Iceland to Akureyri, a town on the Eyjafjörður fjord.

Die majestätische Natur im Norden Islands ist das prägende Thema der zweiten Etappe. Das Land ist äußerst dünn besiedelt, hier oben finden sich nur wenige kleine Städte, in den meisten Fällen leben die Bewohner des Nordens in Dörfern und Gehöften. Dass Island aus vulkanischer Tätigkeit entstanden ist, spürt man in diesem Winkel der Insel jederzeit: Die Kegel von Vulkankratern, heiße Quellen, bizarre Tuff- und Basaltgebilde finden sich überall, manche Gegenden sind vom Schutt der Eruptionen bedeckt und nur sparsam von Vegetation überzogen. Alte Lavaströme durchziehen das Land, die Erdkruste ist zerborsten und aufgeworfen, Flussläufe stürzen sich immer wieder als gischtende Wasserfälle über hohe Felsstufen. Nach den unzähligen Fjorden des Westens lassen wir die zerklüftete Küste Islands bei Akureyri hinter uns zurück und folgen der isländischen Ringstraße auf ihrem Weg durchs Landesinnere. Selbstverständlich gehören aber auch die abseits liegenden Naturwunder zur Etappe. Erst im Tal des mächtigen Lagarfljót, der sich hier zum Meer im Norden schiebt, endet bei Egilstaðir unsere Etappe.

The majestic natural phenomena in the north of Iceland are the defining theme of the second stage of our journey. The country is extremely sparsely populated and there are only a few small towns at these latitudes. For the most part, the northern population live in villages and small settlements. In this part of the island, you never forget that Iceland was created from volcanic activity: the conical forms of volcanic craters, hot springs, bizarre tufa and basalt structures can be found everywhere. Some areas are covered by the debris from the eruptions and only feature sparse vegetation. Ancient lava flows crisscross the country. The earth's crust is pitted and shattered. Rivers constantly plunge over high rock faces as foaming waterfalls. After the countless fjords of the west, we leave the rugged coast of Iceland behind at Akureyri and follow the Icelandic orbital route into the interior. Of course, the country's remote natural wonders also form part of this stage. This stage finally ends in Egilstaðir in the valley of mighty Lake Lagarfljót, which presses northward here toward the sea.

3 ETAPPE STAGE

4 ETAPPE STAGE

Eine Welt aus Wasser und Bergen – das sind die Fjorde im Osten Islands. Geformt vom Feuer aus dem Bauch der Erde und dem Gewicht der Eiszeitgletscher strahlt dieses Land eine erhabene und immer wieder auch martialische Urgewalt aus. Die kleine Stadt Seyðisfjörður im gleichnamigen Fjord strahlt eine eigenwillige Ruhe aus, sie ist bis zum Bau des geplanten Tunnels nur im Sommer über den vorgelagerten Gebirgspass zu erreichen. Je weiter man danach an den Fjorden entlang nach Süden fährt, desto beeindruckender wird die Landschaft: In den Himmel ragende Küstengebirge fallen steil zum Meer hin ab, der Nordatlantik brandet gegen einen schwarzen Strand und einen schmalen Streifen Land. Vom Vulkan Vätnajökull streben dann in der Gegend vor Höfn mächtige Geröllflüsse in Richtung Meer, sie sind im Winter eisbedeckt und ähneln im Sommer mit ihren Felsen und Gesteins-Betten den Gebirgsbächen der Alpen – nur ins Hundertfache vergrößert. Eine Landschaft voller Gewalt und Größe eben. In Höfn haben wir dann wieder die Südküste Islands erreicht.

The fjords of eastern Iceland are a world of water and mountains. Formed by fire from the bowels of the earth and the weight of Ice Age glaciers, this country exudes a sublime and constantly martial elemental force. The small town of Seyðisfjörður in the fjord of the same name has an idiosyncratic tranquility. Until the planned tunnel is built, it can only be reached in summer over the mountain pass. The further south you drive along the fjords, the more impressive the landscape becomes: sky-high coastal mountains drop steeply towards the sea. The North Atlantic crashes against a dark beach and a narrow strip of land. Mighty rivers of scree flow from the Vätnajökull volcano toward the sea in the area in front of Höfn. These are covered in ice in winter and, with their rocks and stone beds, resemble the mountain streams of the Alps in summer – only a hundred times bigger. This is a landscape full of violence and grandeur. In Höfn we touch the south coast of Iceland once again.

Nach einem Start in Höfn, einer der größeren Städte an der Südküste Islands, führt uns die letzte Etappe direkt am Fuß der riesigen Vulkanmassive des Vatnajökull und Myrdalsjökull entlang. Die Natur ist geprägt von vielfältigen Schauspielen und eigentümlicher Faszination, Island zeigt wieder einmal sein vulkanisches Gesicht. Die Dramatik dieser Landschaft inspiriert Filmemacher und Fotografen aus der ganzen Welt, so kennt man zum Beispiel die Jökulsárlón-Lagune aus James-Bond-Filmen oder Werbespots. Immer wieder übernimmt die Natur auch selbst Regie, wird zum Hauptdarsteller und zum Drehbuchschreiber. So ist vor allem der Vulkanausbruch des Eyjafjallajökull Ende März 2010 wohldokumentiert, als über Tage hinweg der Flugverkehr über dem Nordatlantik durch in die Atmosphäre geschleuderte Aschewolken zum Erliegen kam. Bei einem Besuch des Landesinneren wechseln wir auf robustes und geländegängiges Gerät und schaffen es so bis zum Vulkan Hekla und an die heißen Quellen von Landmannalaugar. Südlich von Reykjavík kommen wir wieder in dichter besiedelte Gegenden, ein letzter Bogen um die südwestliche Landzunge Islands führt uns zurück in die Hauptstadt und an den Beginn unserer Reise.

Starting in Höfn, one of the larger towns on the south coast of Iceland, the last stage takes us right to the foot of the huge volcanic massifs of Vatnajökull and Myrdalsjökull. Iceland's natural beauty is shaped by diverse spectacles and exerts a peculiar fascination. The island's volcanic face is there for all to see. The drama of this landscape has inspired filmmakers and photographers from all over the world. For example the Jökulsárlón lagoon is familiar from James Bond movies and commercials. Again and again, nature itself takes over as director, leading actor and scriptwriter. In particular, people will remember the volcanic eruption of Eyjafjallajökull at the end of March 2010, when air traffic over the North Atlantic came to a standstill for days due to ash clouds thrown into the atmosphere. When exploring the interior of the country, we switch to a robust, all-terrain vehicle that takes us to the Hekla volcano and the hot springs of Landmannalaugur. South of Reykjavík we find ourselves back in more densely populated areas, completing one last arc around Iceland's southwestern headland, which leads us back to the capital and to where our journey began.

NESJAVELLIR

EDITORIAL

Millionen Kubikkilometer Wasser. Schwarzgrau und kalt, bedrohlich und lebensspendend, eisumkränzt und sturmzerfurcht. Das ist der Nordatlantik. Wale ziehen durch die Weiten, riesige Heringsschwärme folgen immer noch uralten Routen. Am Meeresgrund türmen sich schroffe Gebirge ohne Tageslicht in weiten Ebenen, durch die sich eine gigantische Narbe zieht: Am mittelatlantischen Rücken drängen die Gesteinsplatten Eurasiens und Nordamerikas auseinander, machen den Weg frei für Magma aus dem Erdinneren, das wie glühendes Blut des Planeten hervorquillt und die Rinne stetig verschließt, vernarbt und verkrustet. Rund 1.200 Kilometer südöstlich von Grönland zackt diese tektonische Spalte durch den Meeresgrund, an einer Stelle hat sich das erkaltende Gestein aus dem Erdinneren bis zur Oberfläche des Atlantiks aufgetürmt. Und dort Land geschaffen. Rauchend und schwarz, Heimat für Heimat für Vulkane in der Weite des Meeres. Island.

Die Insel ist rund 100.000 Quadratkilometer groß, ihre Berge reichen über zwei Kilometer hoch in den Himmel am nördlichen Polarkreis und das muss gereicht haben, um von Seefahrern entdeckt zu werden. Als Unruhegeister des Nordens zogen die Wikinger von Skandinavien aus in alle Richtungen der Welt, prügelten sich in einer heute beinahe unverständlichen Hartnäckigkeit mit den Elementen des Meers, zogen durch eine Welt voller Geheimnisse. Die riesige Vulkaninsel im Atlantik könnte zu Beginn ihrer Fahrten ein Ort zum Überwintern gewesen sein, majestätische Landmarke ebenfalls – und dann irgendwann auch Wohnort. Karg und schroff und abweisend. Das Land sagt viel über das Wesen seiner ersten Bewohner. Vielleicht zog aber auch das auf Island etablierte System des Godentums die Wikinger-Meeresnomaden nach Westen: eine Art Mischform aus Demokratie und Monarchie, bei der einander gleichgestellte Gebietshäuptlinge die Interessen ihrer Gemeinschaften zu vertreten hatten. Den Namen der gesetzgebenden

The North Atlantic: millions of cubic kilometers of black-gray water. Cold and threatening, wreathed in ice and wracked by storms, yet teeming with life. Whales roam the vast ocean expanses; huge schools of herring still follow routes established eons ago. On the seabed, craggy mountains rise up in a midnight world of wide plains split asunder by a gigantic chasm. The tectonic plates of Eurasia and North America push apart here on the mid-Atlantic ridge, clearing a path for magma from the earth's core to gush like the hot lifeblood of the planet from wounds that are constantly healing over to form encrusted scars. Around 1,200 kilometers south-east of Greenland, this fault breaks through the seabed, causing the cooling rock from the interior of the earth to pile up to the surface of the Atlantic and creating dry land. This smoking and black volcanic domain in the vastness of the sea is the place we call Iceland.

The island covers around 100,000 square kilometers and its mountains reach over two kilometers high into the sky in the Arctic Circle. This made it substantial enough to be discovered by seafarers in the past. Starting from Scandinavia, the Vikings set out in all directions, wreaking havoc in their wake, battling the sea with a tenacity that is almost incomprehensible today as they explored a world full of mystery. To begin with, they may have used the huge volcanic island in the Atlantic Ocean as a place to overwinter during long voyages – as well as a majestic landmark – and then at some point it also became a place to call home. Barren, rugged and forbidding, the country tells us a great deal about the nature of its first inhabitants. It may be that the system of government established in Iceland also attracted the Viking marine nomads to the west: a kind of hybrid form of democracy and monarchy, in which equal regional chiefs represented the interests of their communities. The modern Icelandic legislative assembly still bears the Norse name Althing, although the chieftains of the past have been replaced with

Versammlung – Althing – trägt das isländische Parlament heute noch, aus den Häuptlingen oder Goden sind sozusagen die Abgeordneten der Neuzeit geworden.

Islands Moderne ist eben schon sehr alt. Sie ist keine Errungenschaft, für die man zuerst Jahrhunderte von alten Seilschaften oder Traditionen hätte abschaffen, umkrempeln oder überlisten müssen, sondern entstammt dem unverblümten Pragmatismus der skandinavischen Wikinger-Gesellschaft. Flache Hierarchien, Gefolgschaft für individuell erfolgreiche Anführer und nicht für alteingesessene Eliten, Interessenausgleich innerhalb der Gemeinschaft statt kollektive Befriedigung der Interessen einiger Weniger – all das ist in der isländischen Gesellschaft in seinen Grundzügen bereits einige hundert Jahre alt. Wer durch die Mordsee ans Ende der Welt fährt, hat eben kaum Toleranz für das Versagen vermeintlicher Eliten. Das mag etwas pathetisch klingen, dürfte aber tatsächlich eine der Grundlagen für den heutigen Charakter der isländischen Gesellschaft sein. Auf Island pflegt man das Gemeinwesen ebenso sorgfältig, wie einen ausgeprägten Individualismus. „HU", sagt der Isländer, 300.000 Stimmen wie Eine, das ultimative Wir-Gefühl, das es auch gibt, wenn gerade keine elf Leute einem Ball hinterher laufen – und jeder Einzelne will dich einen Moment später kennenlernen, ganz lässig und glaubhaft vom Wir zum Du wechseln. Ungemein herzlich sind die Leute hier oben, sie lachen gerne und helfen dir, sich, einander.

Und noch eine weitere Beobachtung ist auf Island zu machen, besonders in der Hauptstadt Reykjavík: Island hat internationalen Charakter. Die ewige Unruhe der Wikinger scheint immer noch in den Isländern umzugehen, die Jungen treibt es mit Macht von der Insel, aber nach Karrieren in Los Angeles, Hongkong oder London ruft es sie wie Zugvögel zurück in den Norden. Von dort bringen sie die Welt mit nach Island. Musiker, Köche, Architekten, Künstler. Reykjavík ist sozusagen der kleine Underground-Club des Planeten, in dem Weltstars gastieren. Das macht etwas mit der Stadt, das macht etwas mit Island, das kulturelle Magnetfeld der Erde verschiebt sich so nach Norden: Während es früher hinter Glasgow oder Oslo ruhig wurde, hat der Aufstieg Reykjavíks den Puls des Nordens rasant beschleunigt. Die Oberfläche des Nordatlantik wirft Wellen. Besonders die Gastro-Szene Reykjavíks profitiert von dieser Synapse in die große,

Völlig hypnotisiert vom 360-Grad-Cinema-scope-Erlebnis dieser Landschaft treibst du dahin, mit hoffnungslos überforderten Synapsen, die sich vergebens an der Einordnung aller Eindrücke versuchen und dann irgendwann glücklich schmelzen.

Mesmerized by the 360-degree cinemascope experience of the landscape, you drift along with your mind blown, trying vainly to classify all your impressions.

today's parliamentary representatives. Iceland's modernity is actually very old indeed. It is not the result of revolution or the abandonment of centuries of tradition, but rather a remnant of the blunt pragmatism of Scandinavian Viking society. Horizontal social structures and an instinct to follow individually successful leaders rather than long-established elites, balancing the welfare of the community against the special interests of the minority, are principles that are several hundred years old in Icelandic society. Anyone who risks voyaging through the murderous North Sea to the ends of the world is unlikely to tolerate the failure of supposed elites. It may sound a little fanciful, but it could be argued that this is one of the foundations on which modern Icelandic society is built. In Iceland, community is cultivated just as carefully as profound individualism. The Icelanders raise their 300,000 voices as one in the 'Huh' chant that took the Euro 2016 championship by storm in the ultimate expression of cohesion. You experience it immediately during an impromptu football game, when everyone wants to get to know you, making you feel part of the gang. The people up here are incredibly warm, like to laugh and are always ready to lend a helping hand.

One more observation about Iceland, especially the capital Reykjavík: its international character. The Vikings' eternal restlessness still seems to linger among Icelanders and young people leave the island in droves, only to return like migratory birds after successful careers in Los Angeles, Hong Kong or London. From there these musicians, chefs, architects and artists bring the world back with them to Iceland.

weite Welt, das Denken der besten Köche landet an den Kochtöpfen hoch oben im Norden Europas. Der Stoff, aus dem die moderne isländische Küche gestrickt ist, besteht zwar nach wie vor aus traditionellen Zutaten und Rohstoffen, aber die Finesse und Leidenschaft des Kochens stammen von weit her. Übrigens dürfen seit einigen Jahren neben Rüben und Kartoffeln durchaus auch Tomaten als typisch isländische Zutaten gelten, man pflanzt die wärmeliebenden Nachtschattengewächse in Gewächshäusern an, die mit Geothermie beheizt sind – die Hitze des Erdinneren unter Island wird so zum Wachstums-Turbo für Tomaten. Natürlich sind Fische ein Hauptelement der isländischen Küche, egal ob es Lachse, Kabeljau und Hering aus dem Nordatlantik sind, Harðfiskur, der beliebte Trockenfisch, den man bevorzugt mit Brot und Butter serviert, oder die Süßwasserfische der isländischen Seen. Nahezu denselben Status hat Lammfleisch – schließlich leben auf Island mehr Schafe als menschliche Einwohner – und man genießt dieses „Hangikjöt" besonders gern geräuchert. Geht es um Geflügel, halten sich die Isländer lieber an Enten und Gänse. Hühner sind eben keine Freunde des rauen Klimas am Polarkreis.

Darüber hinaus darf man sich auf einer kulinarischen Entdeckungsreise aber auch nicht über einen Papageientaucher auf dem Teller wundern, die Seevögel mit dem charakteristisch leuchtenden, großen Schnabel gelten als Delikatesse. Damit wären wir nun auch schon bei den eher ungewöhnlichen Zutaten angelangt: Pferdefleisch und Walfleisch sind anderswo auf der Welt äußerst umstritten, auf Island aber durchaus noch üblich. Fermentierter Hai hat es von der isländischen Traditionsspeise zum Gruselmoment in Reiseführern geschafft und befindet sich dort in bester Gesellschaft mit gekochtem Schafskopf oder in Molke eingelegten Hammel-Hoden. Leibspeisen dieser Kategorie haben ihre Existenz freilich früheren Zeiten zu verdanken, in denen es frische Nahrungsmittel nur während der Sommermonate nach Island geschafft haben und man daher auf Eingelegtes, Fermentiertes und restlos Verwertetes angewiesen war. Man spült solch exquisite Kulinarik-Höhepunkte am besten mit einem Schuss Branntwein hinunter, der Íslenskt Brennivín ist zumindest für den fermentierten Hai ein verlässlicher Begleiter.

Reykjavík is like the world's underground club, where global superstars make guest appearances. This has an effect on the city and on Iceland as a whole. The earth's cultural magnetic field is shifting northwards: while in the past things tended to go quiet beyond Glasgow or Oslo, the rise of Reykjavík has set the pulse of the north racing, making waves on the surface of the North Atlantic.

The foodie scene in Reykjavík is a particular beneficiary of this link with the big, wide world, as the ideas of the world's best chefs end up in the kitchens of Europe's far north. Modern Icelandic cuisine still centers on traditional ingredients and raw materials, but the finesse and passion of its cooks come from much further away. Incidentally, in addition to beets and potatoes, tomatoes have also been a typical Icelandic ingredient for some years now; the heat-loving plants are grown in greenhouses heated using geothermal energy. Thus, the heat from the earth's core under Iceland enables tomatoes to flourish. Of course, fish, whether salmon, cod or herring from the North Atlantic, is a key element in Icelandic cuisine, as is Harðfiskur, the popular dried fish usually served with bread and butter, or the freshwater fish of the Iceland's lakes. Lamb is almost equally popular - after all, Iceland has more sheep than people – and smoked "hangikjöt" is a particular treat. When it comes to poultry, Icelanders prefer duck and goose. Chickens don't do well in the harsh climate of the Arctic Circle.

If you take a voyage of culinary discovery, don't be surprised to find a puffin on your plate. These seabirds with their characteristic large brightly-colored beaks are considered a delicacy. Which brings us to some of the more unusual ingredients found here: horse and whale are extremely controversial elsewhere in the world, but are still commonly served meats in Iceland. Once a traditional Icelandic dish, fermented shark has now gained horror story status in travel guides, along with boiled sheep's head or sheep's testicles pickled in whey. Traditional foods like this owe their existence to earlier times, when fresh food only made it to Iceland in the summer months. At other times of the year, the population depended on pickled and fermented ingredients and animals were consumed from tail to snout. Such exquisite

All das ist dir zu hart? – Auch dann hat Island etwas zu bieten: die Lummur-Pfannkuchen, Kleinur-Schmalzkringel oder luftig dünnen Pönnukökur-Crepes zum Beispiel, dazu den immer mehr auch im Süden bekannten Skyr: eine Art Magerquark, der auf Island besonders gern mit Beeren gesüßt gegessen wird. Spätestens jetzt bist du bereit für die grundlegenden Härten des Landes, die sich vor allem beim Autofahren bemerkbar machen: Allzu zivilisationsnahes Material leidet besonders auf den Schotterpisten des Nordens, Ostens und Landesinneren unermesslich – und zwar zusammen mit dem Fahrer. Hartes Material mit Nehmerqualitäten ist gefragt: Es müssen nicht unbedingt die Ballonreifen der isländischen, gletschergängigen Hardcore-Prügel sein, aber Allradantrieb, etwas erhöhte Bodenfreiheit und ein gewisses Desinteresse an Auto-kosmetischen Aggregatzuständen zwischen „sandgestrahlt", „übel zerschunden" und „völlig im Eimer" helfen auf Island entscheidend weiter.

Erst dann schafft man es in die wilden Winkel Islands, dorthin, wo das Land tatsächlich seine Seele zeigt. Und abfärbt auf die menschliche Seele, wie ein 100.000 Quadratkilometer-Reset-Knopf, der alles in einem auf den Nullpunkt bringt, menschliche Hybris auf Normalmaß zurückführt. Völlig hypnotisiert vom 360-Grad-Cinemascope-Erlebnis dieser Landschaft treibst du dahin, mit hoffnungslos überforderten Synapsen, die sich vergebens an der Einordnung aller Eindrücke versuchen und dann irgendwann glücklich schmelzen.

Realer Taktgeber und roter Faden jeder Erzählung ist hier oben die Natur. Das brütende Tageslicht des Sommers und seine feuchte Kühle, der Regen, die humorlose Klammheit. Warme Tage sind ein Privileg, keine statistische Wahrscheinlichkeit. Und dann ist da ein paar Wochen später wieder die alles konsumierende Dunkelheit des Winters, wenn Eis und Schnee sich wie ein nicht wegzudiskutierender Grund-Akkord in jede Stimmung mischen und jeden Ton angeben. In dieser Welt leben Elfen und andere Wesen, davon sind die Isländer tief überzeugt. Trotz aller Moderne. Und wer einmal auf der Insel unterwegs war, ist sich am Ende nicht sicher, ob das alles nur Aberglaube ist. Da ist etwas. Es gibt keine Worte dafür. Nur das: Island.

culinary delights are best washed down with a shot of brandy, and Íslenskt Brennivín is a reliable companion drink, at least for the fermented shark.

Is all of this a bit too much for you? – Not to worry, as Iceland has other things to offer: pancakes, fritters or airy thin crepes, for example, as well as skyr, which is gaining popularity elsewhere. This is a kind of low-fat quark, which is particularly popular in Iceland sweetened with berries. By now you will be prepared for the basic hardships of life in the country, which are especially noticeable when driving a car: anything too dainty suffers immeasurably, especially on the gravel roads of the north, east and inland – the same goes for the driver too. Tough, hard-wearing materials are the order of the day: you don't necessarily need the balloon-like tires of Iceland's hardcore glacier-going vehicles, but all-wheel drive and higher-than-average ground clearance certainly help. You'll also have to abandon any concern for your car's good looks, as general appearance here ranges from "sandblasted" and "badly bruised" to "complete disaster".

The car is the only way to make it to the wild corners of Iceland, where the country shows its true character. This also rubs off on the human soul, acting like a 100,000 square kilometer reset button that reduces everything to zero and puts human pride back in its place. Mesmerized by the 360-degree cinemascope experience of the landscape, you drift along with your mindblown, trying vainly to classify all your impressions. The real timekeeper and common thread for every story up here is nature itself – the brooding daylight of summer and its damp coolness, the rain, the relentlessly clammy conditions. Warm days are a privilege here, not a statistical probability. And then, just a few weeks later, everything returns to the all-consuming darkness of winter, when ice and snow join in a bass chord that cannot be ignored, defining every mood and setting every note. Despite their modern outlook, the Icelanders firmly believe that elves and other beings inhabit this world. Anyone who has ever visited the island will agree that you can't be sure that this is all just superstition. There is something to it. There is just one word to encapsulate it all: Iceland.

FROSTASTADAVATN

SEYDISFJÖRÐUR

HVERARÖND

JÖKULSÁRLÓN

HEIDAVATN

JÖKULSÁRLÓN

ROAD TO GRINDAVIK

WESTFJORDS

NESJAVALLAVEGUR

ÞÓRISVATN

F 985 JÖKLASEL

MAELIFELL

FAGRADALSFJALL

SVÍNAFELLSJÖKULL

LANDMANNALAUGAR

NESJAVELLIR

REYKJAVIK AKUREYRI

1.553 KM • 33 STUNDEN // 965 MILES • 33 HOURS

Reykjavík. Hier beginnt Island. Die Hauptstadt Islands ist das Tor zur Insel, anders als durch dieses Nadelöhr kommt man kaum auf den eigensinnigen Planeten im Nordatlantik. Es gibt sie zwar, die kleinen Hafenstädte und Landepisten überall auf der Insel und entlang der zerklüfteten Küstenlinie, aber sie alle dienen eher der Industrie, der Fischerei, dem Inlands-Verkehr.

—

Reykjavík is where Iceland begins. Iceland's capital is the gateway to the island and is just about the only way to reach this independently-minded outpost in the North Atlantic. Although the country has several small ports and landing strips dotted all over the island and along the rugged coastline, these mostly serve local industry, fishing and internal travel.

BLAFJALLAVEGUR

HOTELS

SAND HOTEL
LAUGAVEGUR 34
101 REYKJAVÍK
WWW.KEAHOTELS.IS/EN/HOTELS/
SAND-HOTEL

APOTEK HOTEL
AUSTURSTRAETI 16
101 REYKJAVÍK
WWW.KEAHOTELS.IS/EN/HOTELS/
APOTEK-HOTEL

RESTAURANTS

UMAMI
BORGARTÚN 29
105 REYKJAVÍK
WWW.UMAMISUSHI.IS

RAMEN MOMO
TRYGGVAGATA 16
101 REYKJAVÍK
WWW.RAMENMOMO.IS

ROK
FRAKKASTÍGUR 26A
101 REYKJAVÍK
WWW.ROKRESTAURANT.IS

FISH AND CHIPS VAGNINN
WWW.FISHANDCHIPSVAGNINN.IS

DILL RESTAURANT
LAUGAVEGUR 59, 101 REYKJAVÍK
WWW.DILLRESTAURANT.IS

Reykjavík ist aber nicht nur Start- und Endpunkt der meisten Island-Reisen, sondern auch das Herz der Insel. Mehr als die Hälfte der rund 360.000 Einwohner Islands wohnen hier. Holzhäuser und große Steinhäuser im skandinavischen Stil ziehen sich in ruhigen Passagen durch die Innenstadt, sammeln sich zu vollkommen uneitlen Nachbarschaften und wundern sich über die mit knochentrockenem Pragmatismus durchgezogenen Plattenbau- und Beton-Wohngegenden der Außenbezirke. Das ist rein architektonisch betrachtet die eine Seite Reykjavíks, eine Seite die nach Frittierfett und Kaffee duftet, in der sich Strickwolle-Lädchen neben schrullige, kleine Restaurants reihen. Es könnte auch eine Kleinstadt in Dänemark oder Norwegen. sein. Und auf der anderen Seite hat Reykjavík diese Architektur-Monumente einer ambitionierten Neuzeit, die ein klein wenig aussehen, als wären lange Zeit vor den Wikingern fremde Weltall-Kulturen auf Island gestrandet und hätten dann Reste ihrer interstellaren Fähren zurückgelassen: den brachialen Raketen-Kirchturm der Hallgrímskirkja und das bizarre Glasfacetten-Ungetüm der „Harpa", Reykjavíks ultramoderne Konzert-Halle. Dass die Hallgrímskirkja in ihrem Inneren den bodenständig-kühlen Purismus nordischer Protestanten verströmt, sieht man diesem Heavy-Metall-Gitarrenriff aus Beton nicht an. Und die geschuppte Harpa klirrt vor Kälte, saugt das wenige Licht am Polarkreis ein, tiefgefriert es zu kristallinem Aggregatzustand und haucht es danach wieder aus. Blitzt vor Eis-Energie, schillert und leuchtet, ist das materialisierte Nordlicht.

Der vielfältige Reykjavík-Mikrokosmos steht aber am Beginn einer Fahrt, die uns schon bald in eine Welt führen wird, die nichts von internationalen Trends und Zeitgeistern versteht, nur vom endlosen Ein- und Ausatmen der Zeit und von ganz anderen Geistern. Wir rollen durch Reykjavík, füllen die Tanks für Mensch und Maschine und sind dann nach wenigen Minuten aus der Stadt hinaus. Dem Þjóðvegur 1 in Richtung Osten folgen, Reykjavík gehen dann ganz schnell die Häuser aus. Eine karge Tundra-Landschaft wellt sich links und rechts der Straße, schwarze Bäche strudeln dahin und drängen sich in Schächten unter der Straße hindurch – ein Rest von Zivilisation muss so dicht nach der Stadt ja noch zu spüren sein.

Reykjavík is not just the point where most visits to Iceland begin and end, it is also the beating heart of the island. More than half of Iceland's approximately 360,000 inhabitants live there. Wooden dwellings and large Scandinavian style stone houses are lined up along quiet thoroughfares in the city center or clustered together in modest neighborhoods, while the prefabricated, concrete structures of the residential areas on the city's outskirts are a miracle of bone-dry pragmatism. From a purely architectural perspective, this is just one side of Reykjavík, a side that smells of deep-fried food and coffee, where wool shops line up next to quirky, small restaurants. We could be in any small town in Denmark or Norway. On the other hand, Reykjavík also features ambitious, modern architectural monuments that make it look as if alien space travelers became stranded on Iceland long before the Vikings, leaving behind the remains of their starships: the brutal rocket-like church tower of the Hallgrímskirkja and the bizarre glass-faceted "Harpa", Reykjavík's ultra-modern concert hall. You'd never guess from the exuberance of the exterior of the Hallgrímskirkja, which is like a heavy metal guitar riff cast in concrete, that the interior would exemplify the down-to-earth, cool purism of Nordic Protestantism. Likewise, the fish-like scales on the facade of the Harpa building seem to draw in the little amount of light available in the Arctic Circle and blast-freeze it to a crystalline state before releasing it again. It glitters with icy energy, shimmering and shining. The embodiment of northern light.

The diverse microcosm of Reykjavík marks the beginning of a journey that will soon take us to a world that cares nothing about international trends and contemporary fads, focusing instead on the eternal pulse of time and driven by entirely different concerns. We cruise through Reykjavík, grabbing a bite to eat and topping up the gas tank on the way, and a few minutes later we find ourselves heading out of the city. We take the Þjóðvegur 1 route to the east and soon leave the last houses on the outskirts of Reykjavík behind. An inhospitable tundra landscape spreads out in all directions and pitch black streams wind their way in our direction, eventually squeezing through channels under the road – the last signs of civilization as we leave the city behind. As so often, the sky is filled with

Wie so oft ballen sich dichte Wolkenfelder am Himmel, die sich an manchen Stellen zu zerrissenen Fahnen vor blassem Blau auflösen und in der Ferne rumpeln niedrige Berge gegen diesen Himmel an. Grau und braun und schwarz, dorthin wollen wir. Zum Bláfjöll-Gebirge, das seinen Namen heute ganz zu Unrecht trägt. Blau sind die Berge nämlich nicht. Vielleicht meinen die Isländer den Dunst davor oder den Himmel darüber, man hat auf Island nämlich eine heimliche Liebe für sprachliche Blumigkeit und Extrawürste. Germanische und englische Sprachen etwas weiter im Süden haben sich über die Jahrhunderte zu funktionaler Knappheit abgeschliffen, die Isländer nutzen immer noch eine kaum aufgefrischte Form des Altnordischen, die nebulöse, gestelzte, manchmal prahlerische und manchmal wunderschöne Sprache ihrer Wikinger-Vorfahren. Isländisch, das ist das Arabisch des Nordens. Weshalb etwas ganz direkt sagen, wenn man es verklausulieren kann. „Braun" – wie die blauen Berge nämlich in Wirklichkeit sind, es sei denn, es ist Winter und sie sind weiß – klingt einfach nicht so romantisch wie „Blau".

Aber was wissen wir schon über die Isländer? Was kann man schon über dieses Land wissen? Denken wir, als wir oben am Fuß des Bláfjallahorn stehen, das mit seinen rund 700 Metern Höhe für isländische Verhältnisse eigentlich noch kein richtiger Berg ist. Aber weil es nur knappe 40 Kilometer vom Stadtzentrum Reykjavíks entfernt ist und man hier oben herrlich Skifahren kann, ist das Bláfjallahorn eben der Hausberg Reykjavíks. Zwei herrliche Serpentinen werfen sich in seine Flanke und das ist unser Grund für diesen Antrittsbesuch. CURVES. Sie wissen schon.

Zurück in die Ebene, kurz vor Reykjavík auf die 431 nach Nordosten und nun geht es wirklich los. Lange geradeaus, durch ein Land wie die XXL-Version eines verlassenen Tagebaus. In Vulkan-Zeitaltern ist Island eben noch ein Teenager, da kann man sich schon mal etwas nachlässiger kleiden und gehen lassen, mit ein paar Flechten im Gesicht und nicht weggeräumten Brocken vom letzten Vulkanausbruch in der letzten Woche oder vor drei Millionen Jahren. Muss man ja nicht so eng sehen. Dann geht es den Berg hinauf, weite Rampen nur zum Spaß,

dense clouds. Occasionally these part to reveal torn strips of pale blue and, in the distance, a low mountain range rises up undemonstratively. This gray, brown and black world is where we're headed. They're known as Bláfjöll, the Blue Mountains, but on a day like today their name couldn't seem less appropriate. They certainly aren't blue. Perhaps the Icelanders mean the haze in front of it or the sky above, because Iceland has a secret love of flowery and poetic language. The Germanic and English languages found a little further south have been pared back to functional austerity over the centuries, but the Icelanders still use a barely changed form of Old Norse, the nebulous, quirky, sometimes verbose and sometimes beautiful language of their Viking forebears. Icelandic is like the Arabic if the north. Why you say something directly when you can weave a spell with your words instead. Describing the Blue Mountains as "brown" simply doesn't sound as romantic - even if they are in reality brown, unless it's winter and they're white with snow.

But what do we know about the Icelanders? What can we say with any certainty about this country? Let's think for a moment, as we stand at the foot of the Bláfjallahorn. At around 700 meters, is not a real mountain by Icelandic standards. However, because it is only 40 kilometers from the center of Reykjavík and you can go skiing here, the Bláfjallahorn is regarded as the city's local mountain. There are two magnificent serpentines on its flanks, providing the reason for our first ever visit. CURVES. You know the drill by now.

Back on the flat, just outside Reykjavík on the 431 heading north-east things really start to get interesting. We drive straight on for miles, through terrain reminiscent of an outsized abandoned open-cast mine. In volcanic terms, Iceland is still a relative youngster, so we can forgive it for sloppy dressing and a few untidy boulders that have not been cleared away since the latest volcanic eruption, whether last week or three million years ago. We can let that go because the time has come to set off up the mountain, taking in broad ascents just for fun, travelling alongside the geothermal heating pipes that crisscross the country. The road squeezes a way through rocky cliffs, twisting, lurching,

HOTEL / RESTAURANT

ION ADVENTURE HOTEL
NESJAVELLIR VID THINGVALLAVATN
801 SELFOSS
WWW.IONADVENTURE.IONICELAND.IS

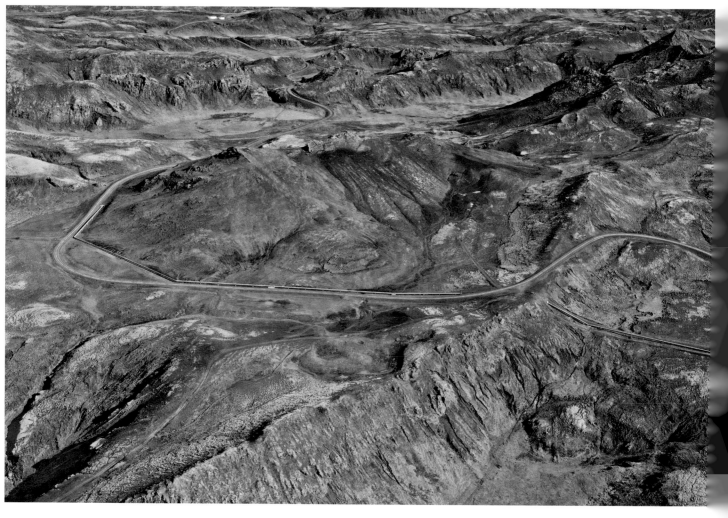

NESJAVALLAVEGUR

HVALFJÖRÐUR

nebenan kreuzen Erdwärme-Rohre durchs Land. Die Straße zwängt sich durch kernige Klippen, kurvt, schlingert, steigt an und fällt ab. Ein wenig fühlt sich das an wie gedreht werden mit verbundenen Augen, nach ein paar hundert Metern weißt du nicht mehr, wo oben und unten ist, Nord, Süd und West. Also weiter auf gut Glück, durch diese Herr-der-Ringe-Landschaft, in der ganz bestimmt Orks und Werwölfe lauern, bis es ganz eindeutig bergab geht. Wir scheinen eine kleine Gebirgskette überwunden zu haben, aber in Wirklichkeit sieht es so einfach aus, wenn die Erdkruste Partylaune hat. Etwas Rock 'n' Roll, etwas Boogie Woogie, ein paar Kilometer lang krachen lassen.

Und jetzt sind wir im Tal des Þingvellir-Nationalparks, einem vulkanischen Graben, in dem einer der größten Seen Islands ruht. Graue Wolken spiegeln sich in der heute glasglatten Oberfläche des Þingvallavatn, der See gibt uns Grüße für seinen wässrigen Nachbarn am Meer mit. Als Hvalfjörður schneidet sich dieser Fjord ins Landesinnere hinein und wir rollen ihm nach unserem Abstecher ins Þingvellir-Tal in energischem Reisetempo entgegen. Wir haben auf unserer ersten Etappe noch einen weiten Weg vor uns, da ist konsequente Fortbewegung wirklich angesagt. Und die Landschaft macht uns das leicht. Sie ist kein verspieltes Element, das nach kleinen Pausen ruft und Ablenkung provoziert, sondern ein stetig gemurmeltes Mantra. Dicht an der Hypnose, mit ungemein dichter Stimmung. Monochrom. Um den Hvalfjörður herum, weiter nach Norden am Meer entlang, bei Borgarbyggð über einen türkisgrauen Sund und weiter, weiter, weiter. Unglaublich lang. Ohne Häuser, Dörfer, Gehöfte. Nur das Land. Ein sprechendes Land. Ein raunendes Land. Mit heiser knirschender Stimme, die bei manchen Tönen kleine Dampfwolken entweichen lässt. Bis zum Gerðuberg fahren wir, umrunden sogar noch die Halbinsel hinaus zum Snaefellsjökull und dringen dann an die Westfjorde im äußersten Norden Islands vor. Die Finger mächtiger Tafelberge greifen hier oben nach dem Nordatlantik. Ihre Ränder fallen zuerst schroff, dann in sanftem Schwung zum Meer hin ab und die Straße schlingert mit Respektabstand zur See dahin. Distanzen verschwimmen: Was bei der Einfahrt in einen Fjord noch überschaubar aussieht,

rising and falling as it goes. After a few hundred meters you lose all sense of direction and can no longer tell which way is up or down, north, south, east or west. We press on through this Middle Earth landscape, where orcs and werewolves probably lurk in wait, until things clearly take a downhill turn. We seem to have crossed a small mountain chain, but in fact it looks like there's a party happening on the earth's crust. For a couple of kilometers it all sounds a little bit rock 'n' roll, a little bit boogie woogie.

We now find ourselves in the valley of the Þingvellir National Park, a volcanic depression that is home to one Iceland's largest lakes. Gray clouds are reflected in the mirror-like surface of Lake Þingvallavatn, a freshwater cousin of the neighboring fjords on the coast. When it becomes the Hvalfjörður fjord, it slices a path inland and, after our detour into the Þingvellir valley, we head toward it at an energetic pace. We still have a long way to go on the first leg of our journey, to we really need to maintain speed. The landscape makes it easy for us. This is no fairytale environment of provoking distractions and tempting stop-offs. Instead it feels like a constantly muttered mantra, a state close to a hypnotic trance. All color is drained from the surroundings of Hvalfjörður, further north along the sea, at Borgarbyggð over a turquoise-gray sound and onward, ever onward. It feels incredibly long. There are no houses, villages or settlements. Just the land. The countryside speaks to you in a whisper, its hoarse, rasping voice releasing small breaths of vapor from time to time. We drive to Gerðuberg, completing a circuit of the peninsula out to Snaefellsjökull and then moving on to the western fjords in the far north of Iceland. Mighty table mountains reach like fingers toward the North Atlantic. Their edges fall first steeply, then in a gentle curve towards the sea and the road winds along at a respectful distance from the sea. Distances become blurred: what looks a modest stretch as you enter a fjord turns into an hour-long drive before you reach the next fingertip. You then find that the next inlet simply eats its way deep inland. Every inch cries out to be explored and only in some cases bridges or dike roads at the flat end span the fjord. Often you have to drive right to the end, until the road crosses a rivulet flowing from the country's interior by an unspectacular

HOTEL / RESTAURANT

HÓTEL BÚDIR
356 SNAEFELLBAER
WWW.HOTELBUDIR.IS

ARNARSTAPI HOTEL
ARNARSTAPAVEGUR, ARNARSTAPI
WWW.ARNARSTAPICENTER.IS

BAULARVALLAVATN

DYNJANDI

wird zu einer stundenlangen Fahrt. Bis zur nächsten Fingerspitze. Nur um dann festzustellen, dass sich dort einfach nur der nächste Meeresarm ins Land hinein-frisst. Und sie alle wollen umrundet sein, nur manchmal überspannen Brücken oder Deichstraßen am flachen Ende den Fjord. Häufig musst du bis ans Ende fahren, bis die Straße ganz unspektakulär als kleiner Betonbogen über ein Rinnsal aus dem Landesinneren hüpft. Der Schweiß der Gletscher und weißen Berggipfel rinnt hier ins Meer, plätschert über Geröll und Steine, löst sich dann im dunkelgrünen Wasser des Fjords auf.

Die Berge gleichen immer wieder titanenhaften U-Booten, die rudelweise am Strand liegen und an imaginären Ankerketten zerren. Je weiter die Straße der zerklüfteten Küstenlinie folgt, desto brüchiger wird sie. Klirrende Winter setzen ihr zu, zerbrechen sie oder lassen erst gar nicht zu, dass sie dem Teenager-Stadium als Schotterpiste entwächst und zur Asphaltstraße reift. Hier oben muss dein Auto Zähne haben, Island wird es sonst sandstrahlen, mit Steinen bewerfen, ruinieren. Grober Schotter knallt in den Radhäusern, die Reifen rattern über Querrillen, die Federelemente des Fahrzeugs und Nerven der Fahrenden werden heiß- und weichgekocht. Und dann, ganz plötzlich, ändert die Straße wieder ihren Aggregatzustand, wird von rau und knochig zu samtig-glatt – aber das täuscht. Allein der Unterschied zwischen Schotterpassagen und Abschnitten auf Asphalt gaukelt diese plötzliche Sanftheit vor. Für sich betrachtet sind die Straßen hier oben immer so Schmirgelpapier-rau wie die Zungen altertümlicher Wikinger-Drachen. Immer weiter strömt der Vestfjarðvegur Nummer 60, die Westfjord-Straße, nach Norden und landet schließlich am letzten großen Meeresarm vor der unzugänglichen Hornstrandir-Halbinsel – der Eisfjordtiefe. Iísafjarðardjúp. In ihrem Inneren gut geschützt vor dem kalten Wasser des Grönlandstroms liegt die kleine Hafenstadt Ísafjörður, sie ist der nördlichste Punkt unserer Fahrt in den Westen Islands. Es wird noch viele Kilometer dauern, bis wir die Fjorde des Nordwestens hinter uns gelassen haben, dann geht es durch die Täler am Fuß der Bergketten des isländischen Nordens bis nach Akureyri. Hier liegt der Hafen unserer ersten Etappe.

Hier oben muss dein Auto Zähne haben, Island wird es sonst sandstrahlen, mit Steinen bewerfen, ruinieren.

Cars need to be tough in these climes, otherwise Iceland will sandblast them into submission.

concrete arch. The meltwater from the glaciers and white mountain peaks runs into the sea here, splashing over scree and stones before it meets the dark green water of the fjord.

The mountains resemble titanic submarines lying in packs by the shore, tugging on imaginary anchor chains. The further we go along the rugged coastline, the more fractured the road becomes. Harsh winter conditions take their toll, breaking up the surface, or even preventing the road from fully maturing into an asphalt highway. Cars need to be tough in these climes, otherwise Iceland will sandblast them into submission. Coarse gravel clatters in the wheel arches. The tires rattle over pitted surfaces. The vehicle's suspension is boiled to jelly – as are the driver's nerves. Then, all of a sudden, the road changes again, turning from rough and bony to velvety smooth. But don't be deceived: it is simply the switch from gravel to sections of asphalt that gives the impression of this sudden gentleness. Taken in isolation, the roads up here are always as rough as the fiery breath of ancient Viking dragons. Vestfjarðvegur, the Westfjord Strait, is national route number 60 pushes further and further north toward the inaccessible Hornstrandir Peninsula, before finally reaching Iísafjarðardjúp, the last major inlet. Within this fjord, well protected from the cold waters flowing down from Greenland, is the small fishing community of Ísafjörður, the most northerly point on our journey into western Iceland. We need to travel a lot further before we leave behind the fjords of the north-west, eventually travelling through the valleys below the mountain chains of northern Iceland to reach Akureyri. This marks the end of the first stage of our trip.

HOTEL / RESTAURANT

ICE APARTMENTS AKUREYRI
HAFNARSTRATI 106
600 AKUREYRI
WWW.ICEAPARTMENTS.IS

RUB 23
KAUPVANGSSTRATI 6
600 AKUREYRI
WWW.RUB23.IS

REYKJAVIK AKUREYRI

Die Hauptstadt Islands steht am Beginn dieser Reise, nicht nur, weil sie das beinahe einzige internationale Tor auf die Insel ist, sondern weil sie viel über Island erklärt. Die Geschichte, die Moderne, das aufgeschlossene und gleichzeitig eigensinnige Wesen der Isländer. Und man kann sich in Reykjavík akklimatisieren, mit einer kleinen Schonfrist auf die Schroffheit Islands einstellen. Von hier aus fahren wir zuerst ein Stück weit ins Landesinnere, besuchen den Þingvellir-Nationalpark und streben dann an der Westküste Islands entlang nach Norden. Eine Runde über die Halbinsel des Snaefellsjökull muss sein, viele Kilometer später landen wir auf der Halbinsel Vestfirðir, die sich mit ihrer von Fjorden zerfurchten Küstenlinie weit hinaus in die Grönlandsee erstreckt. Wir umrunden die sogenannte Westfjord-Halbinsel und machen uns dann im äußersten Norden Islands auf den Weg zu einer Stadt am Eyjafjörður: Akureyri.

—

This trip begins in Iceland's capital, not just because it is almost the only international gateway to the island, but also because it tells us a lot about Iceland: its history and modernity, as well as the open-minded and at the same time stubborn nature of the Icelanders. Reykjavík also offers a chance to acclimatize, a short grace period as you adjust to the ruggedness of Iceland. From here we first head inland, visiting the Þingvellir National Park and then taking off to the north along the west coast of Iceland. A circuit of the Snaefellsjökull Peninsula is not to be missed. Many kilometers later we reach the Vestfirðir peninsula, which stretches far out into the Greenland Sea with its fjord-rutted coastline. We circumnavigate the Westfjord Peninsula and then set off for the far north of Iceland to Akureyri, a town on the Eyjafjörður fjord.

1.553 KM • 33 STUNDEN // 965 MILES • 33 HOURS

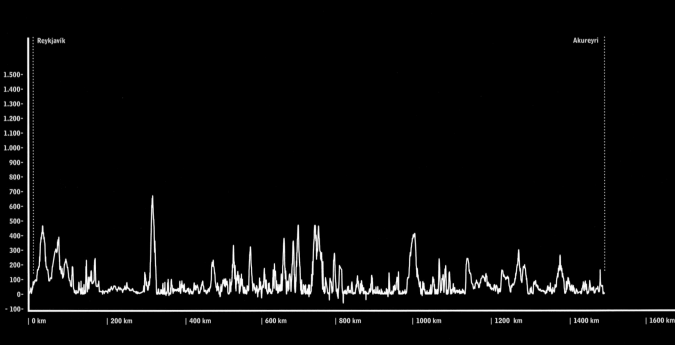

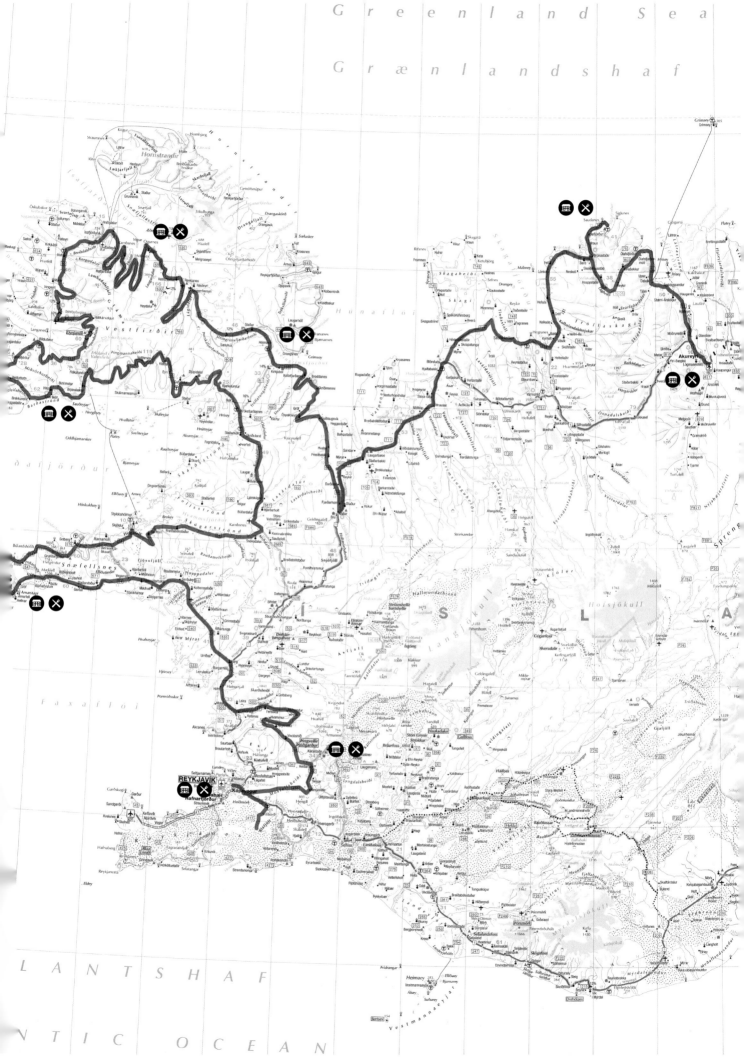

AKUREYRI EGILSTAÐIR

611 KM • 9 STUNDEN // 380 MILES • 9 HOURS

Moosiges Grün bepelzt schwarzgrauen Basalt, durch ein enges Tal strebt ein kleiner Fluss in Richtung Eyjafjörður. An seiner Mündung haben Händler und Hochseefischer eine der nördlichsten Städte Islands gegründet. Akureyri erwischt gerade einen sparsamen Sonnen-Moment, die weite Ebene am Fjord leuchtet grün, wassergraue Wolken-Schlachtschiffe tragen am babyblauen Himmel ein Zeitlupen-Seegefecht aus.

—

A layer of green moss covers the grey-black basalt. A little river passes through a narrow gorge, herrying towards Eyjafjörður. The mouth of this waterway is the place where traders and deep-sea fishermen established Iceland's northern-most town. For a fleeting moment, Akureyri is bathed in sunlight, illuminating the wide expanse of the fjord, as battleship-grey clouds perform endless combat maneuvers against a baby-blue sky.

HOTEL

FOSSHOTEL MÝVATN
GRÍMSSTA IR, 660 SKÚTUSTA AHREPPUR
WWW.ISLANDSHOTEL.IS/HOTELS-IN-
ICELAND/FOSSHOTEL-MYVATN

HÓTEL LAXÁ
OLNBOGAÁS, 660 MÝVATN
WWW.HOTELLAXA.IS

....

RESTAURANT

GAMLI BAERINN
660 REYKJAHLÍD

....

Auf den Kuppen der Berge ringsum hat sich der Schnee des Winters gut gehalten, von dort oben fegt ein stetiger, kühler Wind über die Stadt und sabotiert alle Bemühungen der Sonne, uns die Kleider vom Leib zu ziehen. Riesige Kreuzfahrt- und Fährschiffe lungern im Hafen der Stadt, sie schaffen es ohne Probleme bis hierher ins Landesinnere, obwohl das offene Meer rund 60 Kilometer entfernt am Eingang des Fjords liegt: Die Küste fällt steil zum Grund hin ab, nur wenige Meter vom Strand entfernt ist das Wasser bereits tief und schwarz.

Wir verlassen die Stadt nach Osten hin über den Vaðlaheiðargöng-Tunnel: Der sticht als letzter Gruß menschlicher Zivilisation geradewegs unter dem am Fjord angrenzenden Gebirgszug hindurch – und entlässt uns auf der anderen Seite in ein geradezu magisches Szenario. Wir segeln ins nach Südosten verlaufende Tal hinein, die Sonne eines langen Polartags feuert eine Lightshow durch die Wolken. An den Bergkuppen ringsum haben sich Hochnebelschleier verfangen, aus kleinen Seitentälern wabern wattige Wolkenfetzen. Alles leuchtet, die Welt ist gefüllt mit Licht. Buschwerk und Gras flirrt in allen Grün- und Brauntönen,

The tenacious winter's snow is still clearly visible on the surrounding peaks. From here, a constant cold wind sweeps across the city, sabotaging the sun's efforts to make us peel off a layer or two of clothing. Huge cruise ships and ferries are tied up in the town's port. Even though we're about sixty kilometers from the open sea, these giants can easily make it this far into the country's interior, as the sides of the fjord fall away steeply, so that the water is deep and dark only a few meters from the shore.

We take the eastern route out of town via the Vaðlaheiðargöng Tunnel: as a parting gesture from human civilization, it plunges under the mountains that edge the fjord – and releases us into an almost magical scene on the other side. We find ourselves sailing into a valley stretching towards the south-east, as the polar sun pierces the clouds in a spectacular light show. Veils of mist have become trapped by the surrounding mountain tops and wisps of fluffy cloud are wafted from small side valleys. Everything is alight. The world seems to glow. Shrubs and grasses shimmer in every conceivable shade of green and brown. Tiny flowers form small patchwork carpets that

HVERARÖND

HVERARÖND

HVERARÖND

winzige Blümchen bilden kleine Flicken-teppiche, gerade also ob sie dieses unwirk-liche Universum am Ende der Welt für einen kurzen Moment feierlich dekorieren woll-ten. Eine bedeutsame Sekunde lang dauert dieser Moment – dann sackt wieder alles in monochromes Grau.

Dicht am Ufer des Ljósavatn-Sees entlang führt die Straße, sein dunkles Auge scheint uns gespannt zu verfolgen. Wenige Kilo-meter weiter haben wir den Skjálfanda-fljót erreicht, der als milchig-brauner Strom in Richtung Meer drängt und sich an die-ser Stelle in drei Läufe aufteilt. Parken. Kur-zer Fußmarsch flussaufwärts. Diese Etappe gehört den Naturwundern des Nordens – Nummer eins ist der Goðafoss. Von Weitem ist das Rauschen des Wasserfalls zu hören, dann ein feiner Dunst zu sehen und zu spü-ren. Wie mit dem Zirkel ins Land geschnit-ten quert eine hohe Stufe als Bogen den Lauf des Flusses, das Wasser fällt als weißer, unaufhörlicher Vorhang ins untere Becken. Ob wir die alte Geschichte glauben sollen, nach der die letzten Heidengötter der Wi-kinger hier in den Wasserfall geworfen wurden, um dem Christentum Platz zu machen? – Vermutlich schon. Hier oben halten sich alte Geschichten ausgesprochen gut. Und der Wasserfall strahlt nicht die Endgültigkeit eines Grabes aus, sondern eher den ewigen Kreislauf der Dinge. Thor und Odin dürften ihr Ende im Götterfall Goðafoss gelassen hingenommen haben. Wer weiß schon, was ein paar Meter fluss-abwärts dann doch wieder aus den Fluten steigt?

Zurück zur Straße, zurück nach Norden. Der kleine Abstecher nach Húsavik muss sein, im kleinen Fischerstädtchen an der Küstenstraße 85 finden sich gleich drei Museen, von obskur bis spannend: Wir staunen uns durchs Entdecker-Museum, wundern uns durchs Safnahúsið-Museum der regionalen Besonderheiten und bekom-men auch im Wal-Museum kaum den Mund wieder zu.

Die rund 50 Kilometer bis hinunter zum Mývatn, dem Mücken-See, sollten freilich genutzt werden, um einen gut geschlossenen Normalzustand zu erreichen, denn die vom See aufsteigenden Mückenschwärme werden uns als teilweise regelrecht apokalyptisch

briefly adorn this unreal universe at the end of the world. This moment of delirious beau-ty proves transient and seconds later every-thing is once again bathed in monochrome grey.

The road skirts the shore of dark, brooding Lake Ljósavatn. A few kilometers further on we reach the River Skjálfandafljót, flowing towards the sea in a milky-brown stream and dividing into three separate courses at this point. We park the car and take a short walk upriver. This stage of our jour-ney is dedicated to the natural wonders of the north, first among them Goðafoss wa-terfall. The rushing sound of the cascading torrent can be heard from a distance, be-fore you start to see and feel a fine haze. As if incised into landscape with a compass, a tall, curving step cuts through the course of the river, and the water falls into the basin below like an endless white curtain. Legend has it that the last of the Viking gods were thrown into the abyss here to make way for Christianity. Should we believe the folk-tales? Maybe. After all, the ancient sagas seem quite plausible in this setting. The waterfall seems more like a witness to the eternal cycle of life rather than the finality of death. Thor and Odin may have accepted their fate in the waters of the Goðafoss with a degree of equanimity. Who knows what might be resurrected from the flood a few meters downriver?

But it's time to get back on the road and to continue our northern journey. A short de-tour to Húsavik is a must. The small fishing community on coastal route 85 is home to three museums, ranging from the ob-scure to the awe-inspiring: we find the Museum of Exploration surprising, the Saf-nahúsið-Museum of Regional Curiosities intriguing and the Whale Museum simply astonishing.

The approximately 50-kilometer descent to Mývatn (literally Mosquito Lake) affords us an opportunity to prepare ourselves men-tally: the swarms of mosquitoes that rise from the lake are sometimes described as downright apocalyptic and overwhelming. Today, to our great relief, all is quiet and the buzzing doesn't seem noticeably louder than anywhere else. We decide to take our second substantial break on this stage of

und aufdringlich geschildert. Heute herrscht zu unserer großen Erleichterung allerdings Ruhe, es summt und brummt kaum mehr als anderswo und wir nehmen uns die zweite große Auszeit dieser Etappe. Ziehen zu Fuß an den Seeufern entlang, streunen durch eine Landschaft, die Kulisse eines Fantasy-Epos sein könnte: Felsige Winkel streuen sich in eine grüne Weite, die Wasseroberfläche des Sees scheint von kleinen Inseln und Felszungen übersät zu sein. Dunkle Kegel thronen überall – was so aussieht wie die Einschläge eines Meteoritenschwarms sind allerdings vulkanische Pseudokrater: Auswurf von plötzlichen Wasserdampf-Explosionen, die abgesprengten Deckel unterirdischer Kochtöpfe sozusagen. Wir fahren weiter, umrunden den See, werfen dabei von Weitem einen Blick auf den imposanten Hverfjall-Krater im Osten der großen Wasserfläche und landen dann in den heißen Jarðböðin-Quellen am Fuß des Krafla-Vulkans. Beinahe etwas eingeschüchtert kauern wir im eisblauen, aber dampfenden Wasser und sinnieren über die Urgewalt der Erde unter uns. Sich wohlig räkeln, während einige Kilometer weiter Schlote rauchen, Schlammbecken kochen und die Krater Jahrtausende alter Dampfexplosionen kahl und schwarz in den Himmel ragen, das löst eine sonderbare Mischung aus Demut und Übermut aus. Die Straße zum Krater des Krafla nehmen wir zum Abschied aus dieser Ecke Islands trotzdem, schließlich ist es dieser Vulkan, zu dem all die kochenden Wunder in seinem Einzugsbereich gehören.

Die Straße macht sich dann über ein weites Plateau nach Osten davon, quert den Lauf der Jökulsá á Fjöllum mit einer von der Witterung geprügelten Hängebrücke und stellt uns dann vor eine Entscheidung: Weiter nach Osten fahren oder einen weiteren Abstecher nehmen? Wir entscheiden uns für Letzteres, schließlich ist der Flusslauf der „Jökulsá á Fjöllum" gespickt mit den für Island so typischen, spektakulären Wasserfällen: dem bizarren Selfoss, dem wuchtigen Dettifoss, dem majestätischen Hafragilsfoss und der Kombination aus Réttarfoss sowie dem etwas weiter nördlich in einer tiefen Klamm gelegenen Vigabjarsfoss. Wir fahren also nach Norden, schlagen uns immer wieder auf kleinen Pfaden

our journey. We walk along the shores of the lake, ambling though a landscape like something from an epic fantasy film: rocky outcrops are dotted throughout the vast green expanse. The surface of the lake is scattered with tiny islands and crags. Dark conical forms dominate the landscape. Although they look like the pockmarks of a meteorite storm, they are in fact volcanic pseudo-craters, the remains of sudden explosions of steam, as if the lid has been blown off an underground pressure cooker. We drive on, circumnavigating the lake and enjoying a distant view of the imposing Hverfjall crater to the east, before we reach the Jarðböðin hot springs at the foot of the Krafla volcano. A little intimidated, we cautiously squat in the ice-blue, steaming water and ponder the elemental forces of the earth below us. We experience a strange combination of humility and exhilaration as we lounge about in comfort while a few kilometers away vents smolder, mud pools splutter and the craters from ancient explosions reach towards the sky. Undaunted, we take the road to the Krafla crater as way of saying farewell to this corner of Iceland. After all, this volcano is the reason why all the infernal wonders in the surrounding area exist.

The road traverses a wide plateau to the east, crossing the River Jökulsá á Fjöllum on a storm-tossed suspension bridge. We face a decision: do we drive further east or take another detour? We decide on the latter. We've been told that the course followed by the Jökulsá á Fjöllum includes several of the spectacular waterfalls for which Iceland is renowned: the bizarre Selfoss, the mighty Dettifoss, the majestic Hafragilsfoss and the combination of the Réttarfoss and the Vigabjarsfoss a little further north in a deep ravine. So we head north, veering off again and again onto narrow trails to follow the astonishing path of the river. It takes a few hours to get back to the intersection that allows us to join National Route 1, the Þjóðvegur orbital route. We first take a southerly bearing, subsequently crossing a series of mighty hills of volcanic scree to the east.

Following a final curve to the south, the orbital route reaches Egilstaðir on the shores of the Lagarfljót, which seems uncertain

in Richtung Fluss und staunen. Es dauert Stunden, bis wir wieder zurück an der Abzweigung sind, um der Nationalstraße 1, der Ringstraße, dem Þjóðvegur, weiter zu folgen. Zuerst in südlicher Richtung, dann in der Querung einer mächtigen Hügelkette aus Vulkanschutt nach Osten.

Einem letzten Bogen nach Süden folgend landet die Ringstraße dann bei Egilstaðir am Lagarfljót. Der weiß nicht so recht, ob er Fluss oder See sein will, wir dagegen ganz genau, dass diese Etappe noch einen letzten Abstecher haben wird: am Westufer des Lagarfljót entlang nach Süden, bis zu einem Parkplatz am südlichen Ende des Sees. Nach einer rund anderthalbstündigen Wanderung haben wir zuerst den Litlanesfoss und dann den Hengifoss erreicht. Der zweithöchste Wasserfall Islands stürzt zwischen Basalttürmen in einem derben Gesteinsbruch nach unten, so tief, dass sich der Wasservorhang kurz vor seinem Aufprall beinahe zu einem Nebelschleier auflöst. Beeindruckt treten wir den Rückweg an und fahren weiter. Über ein paar deftige Serpentinen den Berg hinauf und weiter ins Landesinnere. Unser Ziel ist eine Schlucht, die furchteinflößend und eigentümlich schön zugleich ist: Der Hafrahvammagljúfur-Canyon. Interkontinentale Urgewalten haben die Erdkruste hier auseinandergezerrt, das Ergebnis sieht unnatürlich aus, klaffend und grausam. Nahezu senkrechte Felswände fallen tief in die Schlucht hinab, absurd tief: Vielleicht sind es bis zu 200 Meter, und dabei scheint der Riss im Gebirge an manchen Stellen nur wenige Meter breit zu sein. Ein Rinnsal sickert um diese Jahreszeit am Grund mehr dahin, als dass es fließt, der Ort verströmt pure Klaustrophobie und Brutalität. Dass man an den Eingang der höchstens 8 Kilometer langen Schlucht einen Staudamm gebaut hat, dessen Überlauf als betonierte Rinne wie eine Riesen-Kugelbahn am Rand des Canyon endet, verleiht diesem Ort zusätzliche Bedrohlichkeit. Die Natur alleine ist schon brachial, der von Menschen aufgezwungene Zügel verstärkt das noch.

Schweigend fahren wir zurück zum Lagarfljót, wechseln auf seine Ostseite und sind gute anderthalb Stunden nach dem Blick auf den Grund des Hafrahvammagljúfur zurück in Egilstaðir angelangt.

Interkontinentale Urgewalten haben die Erdkruste hier auseinandergezerrt, das Ergebnis sieht unnatürlich aus, klaffend und grausam.

Elemental intercontinental forces have torn the earth's crust apart here. The resulting gaping chasm looks unnatural and horrific.

whether it is a river or a lake. We are experiencing no such doubts because we know that this stage of the trip will involve one final detour: we are going to follow the western shore of the Lagarfljót to the south, to a parking lot at the southern end of the lake.

After a hike of around an hour and a half, we first reach the waterfalls of Litlanesfoss and then Hengifoss. The second highest waterfall in Iceland falls between basalt towers into a rough jumble of rock so deep that the curtain of water almost completely dissolves into mist just before it hits the ground. Suitably impressed, we make our way back to our car and drive on. We negotiate a couple of stiff serpentine bends up the mountain and continue inland. Our destination is a gorge that is both terrifying yet strangely beautiful: the Hafrahvammagljúfur Canyon. Elemental intercontinental forces have torn the earth's crust apart here. The resulting gaping chasm looks unnatural and horrific. Rock walls descend deep into the gorge in an almost vertical drop. It seems almost unfathomable, measuring perhaps up to 200 meters, while in some places the gap in the mountains seems only a few meters wide. At this time of year, only a trickle of water creeps along the bottom rather than the customary torrent. The place exudes a feeling of pure claustrophobia and brutality. The fact that a dam has been built at the mouth of the eight-kilometer gorge, the overflow of which ends in a concrete channel like a gigantic marble run along the edge of the canyon, lends this place an additional eeriness. Nature is brutal enough and the efforts of human beings to harness it seems to amplify this fact even more. We drive back to Lake Lagarfljót in silence, switching to its eastern shore and arriving back in Egilstaðir about an hour and a half after contemplating the profundities of the Hafrahvammagljúfur Canyon.

HOTELS

LAKE HOTEL EGILSSTADIR
EGILSSTADIR 1-2
700 EGILSSTA IR
WWW.LAKEHOTEL.IS

RESTAURANT

NIELSEN RESTAURANT
TJARNARBRAUT 1
700 EGILSSTA IR
WWW. NIELSENRESTAURANT.IS

SECRET WATERFALL
ALONG THE ROAD

AKUREYRI EGILSTAÐIR

Die majestätische Natur im Norden Islands ist das prägende Thema der zweiten Etappe. Das Land ist äußerst dünn besiedelt, hier oben finden sich nur wenige kleine Städte, in den meisten Fällen leben die Bewohner des Nordens in Dörfern und Gehöften. Dass Island aus vulkanischer Tätigkeit entstanden ist, spürt man in diesem Winkel der Insel jederzeit: Die Kegel von Vulkankratern, heiße Quellen, bizarre Tuff- und Basaltgebilde finden sich überall, manche Gegenden sind vom Schutt der Eruptionen bedeckt und nur sparsam von Vegetation überzogen. Alte Lavaströme durchziehen das Land, die Erdkruste ist zerborsten und aufgeworfen, Flussläufe stürzen sich immer wieder als gischtende Wasserfälle über hohe Felsstufen. Nach den unzähligen Fjorden des Westens lassen wir die zerklüftete Küste Islands bei Akureyri hinter uns zurück und folgen der isländischen Ringstraße auf ihrem Weg durchs Landesinnere. Selbstverständlich gehören aber auch die abseits liegenden Naturwunder zur Etappe. Erst im Tal des mächtigen Lagarfljót, der sich hier zum Meer im Norden schiebt, endet bei Egilstaðir unsere Etappe.

—

The majestic natural phenomena in the north of Iceland are the defining theme of the second stage of our journey. The country is extremely sparsely populated and there are only a few small towns at these latitudes. For the most part, the northern population live in villages and small settlements. In this part of the island, you never forget that Iceland was created from volcanic activity: the conical forms of volcanic craters, hot springs, bizarre tufa and basalt structures can be found everywhere. Some areas are covered by the debris from the eruptions and only feature sparse vegetation. Ancient lava flows crisscross the country. The earth's crust is pitted and shattered. Rivers constantly plunge over high rock faces as foaming waterfalls. After the countless fjords of the west, we leave the rugged coast of Iceland behind at Akureyri and follow the Icelandic orbital route into the interior. Of course, the country's remote natural wonders also form part of this stage. This stage finally ends in Egilstaðir in the valley of mighty Lake Lagarfljót, which presses northward here toward the sea.

611 KM • 9 STUNDEN // 380 MILES • 9 HOURS

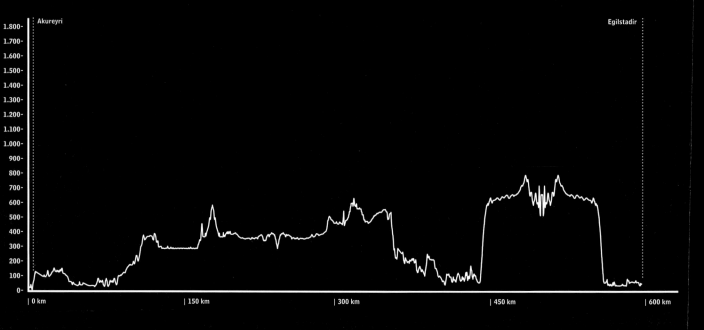

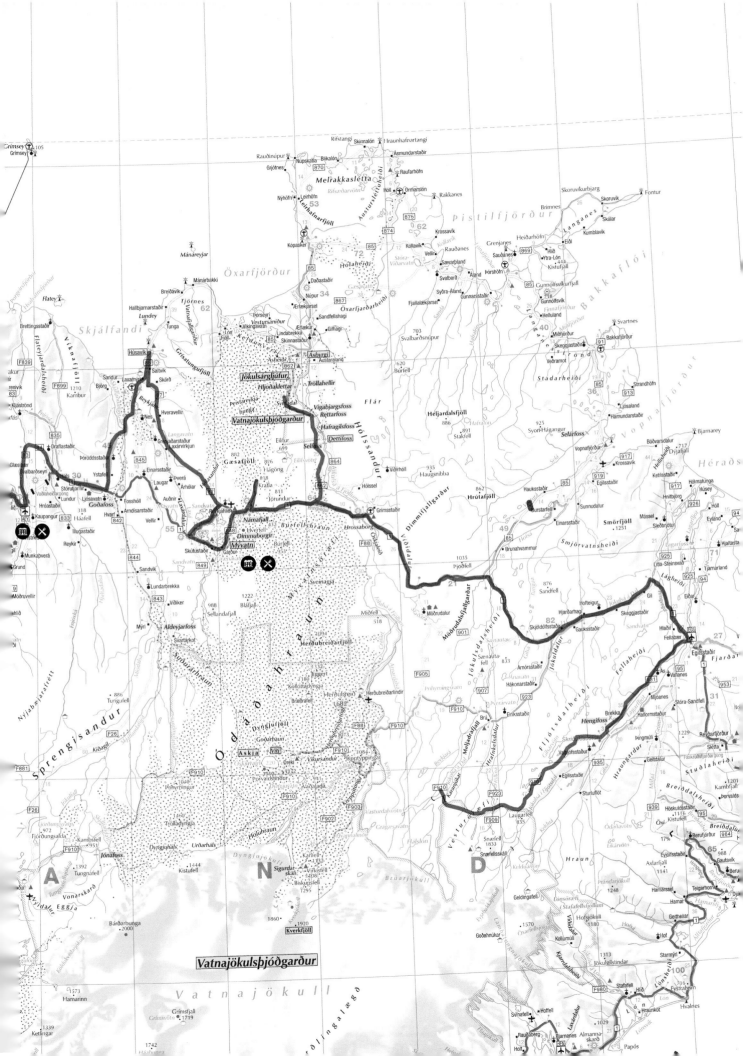

EGILSTAÐIR HÖFN

350 KM • 6 STUNDEN // 218 MILES • 6 HOURS

Ein paar hundert Kilometer Luftlinie weiter westlich, in Reykjavík, treffen sich global-urbaner Lifestyle und die Bodenständigkeit des Nordens zum Engtanz – in Egilstaðir am östlichen Rand Islands kann man sich das kaum vorstellen. Die Kleinstadt am Lagarfljót-Fluss tagträumt unter einem blau-grau gemusterten Himmel, der endlose Tag des Polarsommers hat die Welt fest in seinem Griff.

—

A few hundred kilometers further west as the crow flies, in Reykjavík, the global-urban lifestyle and the down-to-earth attitude of the north meet in a close encounter that is difficult to imagine in Egilstaðir on the eastern edge of Iceland. The small town on the River Lagarfljót dreams the time away under a gray-blue sky, as the endless daylight of the polar summer tightens its grip on the world.

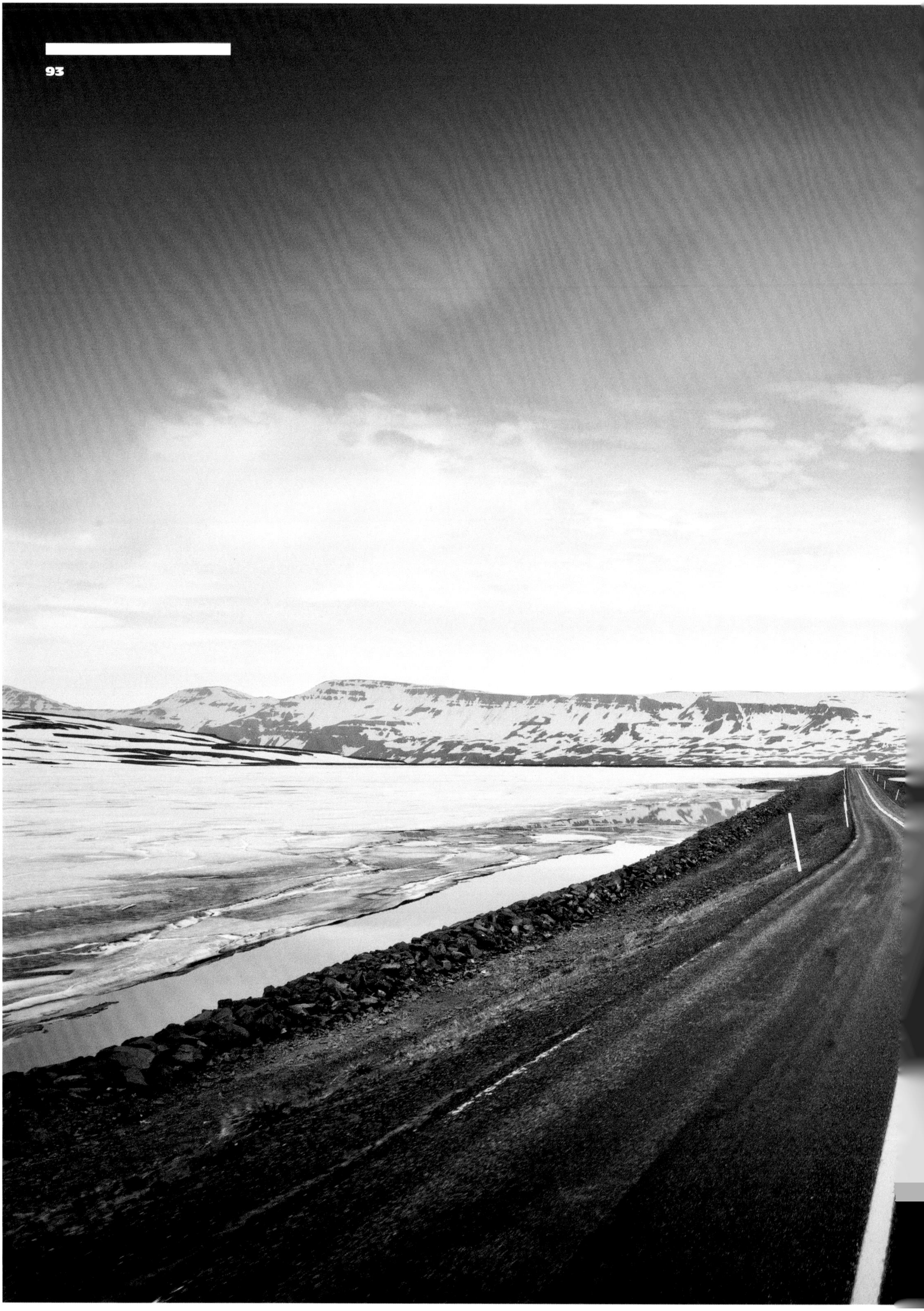

RINGROAD 1

HOTELS

HÓTEL ALDAN
SEYDISFJORDUR
WWW.HOTELALDAN.IS

Bleierne Müdigkeit scheint einen Moment lang alles zu befallen: Autos fahren für einen Augenblick führerlos, Blicke richten sich kurz leer nach innen, Vögel schlagen nicht mehr mit den Flügeln, Insekten summen auf der Stelle. Nur der Wind weht unermüdlich, er ist hier oben das einzige Element ohne Anfang und Ende, ohne Innehalten und Pause.

Die Häuser von Egilsstaðir stehen unschlüssig zwischen dem braungrauen Wasser des Lagarfljót und der Gebirgskette im Osten. Pragmatisch und fantasielos sind sie, ein unbarmherzig realistischer Dämpfer für die Erzählung von cooler, skandinavischer Architektur. Isländische Kleinstädte sind monochrom und banal, ihr uneitler Siedler-Pragmatismus tut aber auch auf eigentümlich demütig machende Weise gut. Das ist alles ein Entwurfsstadium, eine Skizze des Menschen, ein schnörkelloser Serviervorschlag zu den Themen Wohnen, Schlafen, Sein. Nichts mehr. Und irgendwie – gut. Es dauert also trotzdem eine Weile, die Stimmung des Orts hinter sich zu lassen, auch wenn man sich längst über den Seyðisfjarðavegur nach Osten davongemacht hat. Über die karge Tundra und die Weiden im Osten der Stadt, hinauf zur Fjarðarheiði. Weite Rampen ziehen sich den Berg hinauf, die Straße treibt in weiten Bögen voran. Vorbei am Abzweig zum Fardagafoss-Wasserfall, dann hechtet sie in vier, fünf Bögen weiter in Richtung Passhöhe. Weit unten streift ein Sonnenfleck wie ein Theater-Scheinwerfer über die Stadt im Tal, lässt die Ebene kurz grün und braun leuchten, dann ist die Vorstellung beendet. Wir sind im realen Moment angelangt, auf einem groben Asphaltstreifen, der sich der Gipfelkuppe entgegenmüht, begleitet vom monotonen Rhythmus gelber Markierungsstangen. Der nächste Winter wird kommen.

Dann sind wir auf dem Hochplateau angekommen. Wind kräuselt die Oberflächen von Wasserlachen und Tümpeln, die hier oben im Land liegen, wie die Teile eines unvollendeten Puzzles. In Bodenmulden hat sich Schnee gehalten, etwas weiter weg leuchten weiße Bergkuppen. Jemand hat ein Dutzend Betonquader neben die Straße gestellt, bunt bemalt und alte Röhrenfern-

For a moment, leaden fatigue seems to set in: for a moment cars stop moving, thoughts briefly turn inward, birds cease flapping their wings, insects seem to hang motionless in the air. Only the wind blows relentlessly – the only element in these parts that has no beginning or end, no moment of reflection or rest.

The houses of Egilstaðir stand indecisively between the brown-gray water of Lagarfljót and the mountain range to the east. They are pragmatic and unimaginative, a relentlessly realistic rejoinder to the narrative of cool, Scandinavian architecture. Icelandic small towns are monochrome and banal, but their unpretentious settler-style pragmatism also brings you down to earth in a good way. Everything is still at the drawing board stage with practical proposals for human living, sleeping and being. Nothing more. And yet it is all somehow good. As a consequence, it takes a while to leave the atmosphere of the place behind you, even if you have long since made your way east via Seyðisfjarðavegur. We cross the barren tundra and pastures to the east of the city, up to Fjarðarheiði. The road takes a broadly winding route up the mountain. We ignore the turn for the Fardagafoss waterfall, pressing on in four or five arcs toward the top of the pass. Far below, a patch of sunlight sweeps over the town in the valley like a theater spotlight, making the plain briefly shine green and brown. The performance ends as quickly as it began. We are at one with the moment, on a strip of rough asphalt that struggles towards the summit, accompanied by the monotonous rhythm of yellow marker poles, portents of the next winter snows.

We then arrive on the high plateau. The wind riffles the surfaces of puddles and pools that look like pieces of an unfinished jigsaw puzzle. Snow has lingered in hollows, and a little further away, white-covered mountain tops shine brightly. Someone has placed a dozen concrete blocks along the road and painted them brightly to look like old-fashioned television sets. It's probably not art, but we can let that go. There's an Icelander somewhere waiting to see how long it will take before someone notices their work. Onward, ever onward.

95

seher darauf dekoriert. Ist vermutlich keine Kunst, sondern kann weg, und irgendwo wartet ein Isländer, wie lange es dauert, bis das jemand merkt. Weiter, weiter, die Straße hat sich vor nassen Füßen auf einen Deich gerettet, weil die kleinen Wasserlachen-Puzzlestücke sich nun doch zu einem kleinen Gebirgssee verabredet haben. Und dann schaltet die Straße in den Leerlauf, lässt einfach rollen. Zuerst sanft und stetig den Berg hinab, dann in immer steiler werdenden Slalom-Schwüngen. Nebenan versucht ein gischtender Gebirgsbach Schritt zu halten, sprudelt und strudelt und klackert mit Geröll, aber die Straße ist schneller. Zieht davon, reckt die Arme, läuft ins Ziel. Am Seyðisfjörður, der sich hier vom Meer kommend ins Landesinnere hineinzieht und vor den Füßen der gleichnamigen Kleinstadt endet. Trawler und Fähren liegen am Betonkai, denn auch wenn Seyðisfjörður so tut, als sei es das Ende der Welt, ist hier doch ein Tor: Fährschiffe aus Hirtshals in Dänemark fahren mit einem Zwischenstopp auf den Färöer-Inseln bis hier hinauf. Keine Lust mehr auf Island? – Dann wäre jetzt die Gelegenheit für einen unbemerkten Abgang am Hinterausgang. Niemand? – Einverstanden.

Vom äußersten Osten Islands fahren wir zurück über die Berge nach Egilstaðir und dann nach Süden. Geradewegs der Ringstraße 1 folgend, Falllinie in Richtung Äquator. Die Straße pfeilt schnurgerade durch eine mächtige Talrinne zwischen zwei Hügelketten, irgendwann fühlt sich das so an, als würde man stehen und nur die Berge links und rechts vorüberziehen lassen. Dann endet das Cinemascope-Laufband an einer hoch aufragenden Kette aus Bergen, Felsriffen und Hügeln, der Hringvegúr weicht nach Osten hin aus. Hinein in ein breites Tal, das zum Meer hin führt. Einen Moment lang ist das wie Monument Valley meets Schottland meets Alpen, dann sind wir bei Fjarðabyggð am Reyðar-Fjord angekommen. In einem Land uralter Vulkane, über zehn Millionen Jahre alt. Abgehobelt, zermalmt und geschliffen von den Gletschern der letzten Eiszeit. Die Eismassen haben den feuerspeienden Berg-Königen der Urzeit unfassbare 2.000 Meter Höhe genommen, zu Staub und Geröll zermahlen. Wer hier im Landesinneren unterwegs ist,

Although the small pools of water have by now coalesced into a small mountain lake, the road manages to stay high and dry by following a dike. The route then shifts into neutral. At first we find ourselves descending gently and steadily down the mountain, then making increasingly steep slalom turns. Alongside us, a foaming mountain stream tries to keep up, bubbling and gushing. But the road is faster and the car pulls away, stretching out to reach the finishing line at Seyðisfjörður first. This small town is located some distance inland on the fjord. Trawlers and ferries are tied up at the quayside. Although Seyðisfjörður might feel like the end of the world, it is in fact a gateway: ferries from Hirtshals in Denmark dock here, stopping off at the Faroe Islands on the way. Tired of your visit to Iceland? – Here's your chance to skip out by the back door. No takers? – Fair enough. From the eastern edge of Iceland we drive back over the mountains to Egilstaðir and then south on Orbital Route 1, which drops in a straight line toward the equator.

The road cuts like an arrow through a mighty valley gully between two chains of hills. At some point it starts to feel like we're standing still and just letting the mountains pass by to the left and right. The Cinemascope experience ends at a towering chain of mountains, crags and hills, as the Hringvegúr route turns east. We enter a wide valley that sweeps to the sea. For a moment it's like a cross between Monument Valley, the Scottish Highlands and the Alps, then we arrive at Fjarðabyggð on the Reyðar Fjord. We find ourselves in a land of ancient volcanoes, over ten million years old, sliced, crushed and worn down by the glaciers of the last ice age. The ice masses have reduced the fire-breathing volcanic giants of prehistoric times by an unbelievable 2,000 meters, grinding them to dust and rubble. Anyone traveling inland here can read the geology of the region like an open book. Layer after layer can be seen there, shining in every shade from matt black to dark brown and deep red to glassy yellow. It's as if the earth's blood has congealed in icy fire. The mountains that surround the fjord are brutal, like stone polyps stacked on top of each other, seemingly still in motion, rising up to devour one

MUSEUM

FACTORY CAR MUSEUM
SÓLVELLIR
BREIDALSVÍK

liest die Eingeweide der Erde wie ein offenes Buch. Schicht um Schicht liegt da, in allen Schattierungen von mattem Schwarz über starkes Braun und tiefem Rot zu glasigem Gelb leuchtend. Geronnenes Erdenblut, kaltes Feuer.

Die Berge am Fjord sind brachial, wie Polypen aus Stein schichten sie sich übereinander, wirken immer noch wie in Bewegung, quellen auf und verschlingen sich. Zumindest war das einmal so. Man wäre doch zu gern dabei gewesen, als diese Welt einmal aus dem Wasser des Atlantiks auftauchte und sich rauchend, lodernd, feurig formierte. Oder vielleicht besser doch nicht. Bereits das eiskalte Drama des Heute ist respekteinflößend genug. Wenn der Seewind das Wasser des Fjords zu Schaumkronen peitscht und die starren Lava-Monster an seinem Rand schweigend und grausam zusehen.

Die Ringstraße schwingt sich am Südufer des Reyðar-Fjord den Berg hinauf und taucht mit einem letzten Blick zurück aufs Tal in einen Tunnel unter dem Gebirge. Tastet sich dort gerade einmal zweispurig und bei spärlicher

another, as in the past. It would have been amazing to be there to witness this world emerging from the waters of the Atlantic to form itself in a fiery blaze. On second thoughts, perhaps not: today's ice-cold drama is already daunting enough, as the sea breeze whips the water of the fjord into white caps while the cruel lava monsters that line its edge watch in rigid silence.

The orbital route swings up the mountain on the south bank of the Reyðar Fjord and dives through a tunnel under the mountains with a last glimpse of the valley. We grope our way through the twilight interior of the mountain on a two-lane road, emerging in the next fjord valley: the Fáskrúðsfjord. Fishermen from the far south arrived up here at some point, and French street signs and even a French cemetery can be found at Fáskrúðsfjörður, a sign that Iceland is only a stone's throw from mainland Europe or seasoned sea dogs. After all, what are Normans but Northmen? Who knows? We may simply be witnessing the reunification of people who were parted in the long-distant past. We turn to the pressing issue of rest and a bite to eat: good bread and seafood chowder, cod with

RINGROAD 1

HVALNES

Beleuchtung durchs Innere des Berges und hat es so ins nächste Fjord-Tal geschafft: am Fáskrúðsfjord. Fischer weit aus dem Süden sind irgendwann hier oben angekommen, französische Straßenschilder und sogar ein französischer Friedhof finden sich am Fáskrúðsfjörður, als Zeichen, dass Island für harte Seebären vielleicht doch nur in direkter Nachbarschaft zum europäischen Kontinent liegt. Und andererseits: Was sind Normannen denn anderes als Nordmänner? Vielleicht hat sich hier nur gefunden, was zusammengehört? Wer weiß das schon? Viel wichtiger ist jetzt eine kleine Pause, gutes Brot in eine Meeresfrüchtesuppe tauchen, einem Kabeljau beim Rendezvous mit French Fries zu sehen – was kann es Schöneres geben? Vielleicht weiterfahren. Wieder rollen wir dem Land-Ende des Meeresarms entgegen, schwenken dann zum Südufer, dort wartet nun aber kein erneuter Tunnel, mit dem die Berge zu unterqueren wären, sondern der Weg ins nächste Tal muss auf die gute, altmodische Weise absolviert werden: Munter pfeifend geht es vergnügt am Ufer des Fáskrúðs-Fjord entlang, die Straße surft regelrecht dahin, kurvt über die zum Meer hin abfallenden Berghänge und schwingt sich dann in bester Aussichtslage auf den endlosen Nordatlantik ums östliche Ende der Landzunge. Trifft dort bei Austurbyggð auf eine viel kleinere Bucht und dann haben wir den Bogen raus. Die nächsten 130 Kilometer vergehen auf der Küstenstraße wie im Flug. Die Sonne scheint, Schafe grasen mit selbstvergessenem Eifer auf den Wiesen, während der weiße Flaum kleiner Pflanzen im Seewind zittert und so gleich noch einmal Schafherden erscheinen lässt: im Miniaturformat.

Die Berge der nächsten Fjord-Bucht tauchen aus dem Dunst voraus auf und wir fahren ihnen entgegen. Erst als wir den knallig-orangefarbenen Leichtturm von Hvalnes erreicht haben, verändert sich die Szenerie. Über epische Geröllwiesen geht es ein Stück weit ins Landesinnere, die Dimensionen dieser Landschaft sind in solchen Momenten beinahe zu viel für Menschen. Das andere Ende des Tals scheint kaum näherzukommen und die ganze Zeit sind wir begleitet vom Grieseln und Knirschen des Felsschutts um uns herum. Was das Wort

Fischer weit aus dem Süden sind irgendwann hier oben angekommen, französische Straßenschilder und sogar ein französischer Friedhof finden sich am Fáskrúðsfjörður, als Zeichen, dass Island für harte Seebären vielleicht doch nur in direkter Nachbarschaft zum europäischen Kontinent liegt.

Fishermen from the far south arrived up here at some point, and French street signs and even a French cemetery can be found at Fáskrúðsfjörður, a sign that Iceland is only a stone's throw from mainland Europe for seasoned sea dogs.

French fries – what could be nicer? Soon enough the time comes to move on. Once again we drive toward the land end of the fjord, then turn to the south bank. Unfortunately there is no new tunnel waiting to take us through the mountains, so we have to get to the next valley the good, old-fashioned way: whistling cheerfully we take the road along the shores of the Fáskrúðs fjord. We find ourselves literally surfing along, following the curves of the mountains as they slope toward the sea and then swinging around the eastern end of the headland for the best views of the endless North Atlantic. We arrive at Austurbyggð on a much smaller bay and hit our stride. The next 130 kilometers of the coastal road fly by. The sun is shining and sheep graze greedily in the meadows, while white tufts of bog cotton tremble in the sea breeze like herds of miniature sheep.

The mountains of the next fjord rise up from the mist ahead as we drive toward them. The scene only changes when we have reached the bright orange lighthouse of Hvalnes. We drive a little way inland, crossing epic scree fields. The dimensions of this landscape are almost too much absorb at time like this. The other end of the valley never seems to come any closer and the whole time we hear the crunch of the rubble around us in our ears. You begin to understand exactly what the word "erosion" means, as the mountains turn into

RESTAURANT

OTTO MATUR & DRYKKUR
HAFNARBRAUT, HÖFN

....

HOTEL

FOSSHÓTEL VATNAJÖKULL
HORNAFJÖRDUR
781 HÖFN

....

HVALNES

In sicherer Distanz vom offenen Meer hangelt sich die Ringstraße auf einem beinahe behelfsmäßig wirkenden Metallsteg über einen steingrauen Strom zur weiten Fläche eines Flussbetts. Hunderte Meter breit ist es, bedeckt mit Geröll und Schutt, Rinnsale, Bäche und kleine Flüsse durchziehen es. Während der Frühjahrsschmelze müssen hier gigantische Wassermassen aus den Bergen ins Meer fließen und das gesamte Tal überfluten. Breiter als jeder Strom Europas, einfach nur das Sterben von Eis.

Keeping a safe distance from the open sea, the orbital route crosses a slate-gray stream on an almost makeshift metal bridge to reach the wide expanse of a river bed. It is hundreds of meters wide, covered with boulders and rubble, crisscrossed with rivulets, streams and small rivers. During the spring melt, gigantic masses of water flow from the mountains to the sea, flooding the entire valley. Wider than any river in Europe, this is just the last evidence of the death-throes of the winter's ice.

„Erosion" bedeutet: Jetzt meinst du, es zu verstehen. Wenn sich Berge in Wüsten aus Sand und Geröll verwandeln. Soweit das Auge reicht. Wartend auf den nächsten Winter und seine Mühle, die nächste Sturmflut und ihre Urgewalt. In sicherer Distanz vom offenen Meer hangelt sich die Ringstraße auf einem beinahe behelfsmäßig wirkenden Metallsteg über einen steingrauen Strom zur weiten Fläche eines Flussbetts. Hunderte Meter breit ist es, bedeckt mit Geröll und Schutt, Rinnsale, Bäche und kleine Flüsse durchziehen es. Während der Frühjahrsschmelze müssen hier gigantische Wassermassen aus den Bergen ins Meer fließen und das gesamte Tal überfluten. Breiter als jeder Strom Europas, einfach nur das Sterben von Eis.

Ein paar letzte Kilometer noch, dann pilgert die Straße abgekämpft und müde der Stadt Höfn entgegen. Zur Rechten zerfallen riesige Tuffberge zu Geröll, enorme Halden von grauem Gestein rieseln auf den Sockel Islands zu und enden an einem Streifen von Gras und Weiden vor der Küste. Durch diese Weiden hindurch strebt nun die Straße. Wir freuen uns aufs Ankommen, freuen uns über die sanften Wellen des Graslands am Meer, das ein wenig wie die ländliche Idylle Norddeutschlands oder Südskandinaviens wirkt: Wiesen, kleine Gräben und Zäune, dann erste Wohngebiete, die sich hinter Baumreihen ducken. Tankstelle, Arbeiterwohnungen, dann Einfamilienhäuser aus Holz. Grau und quadratisch. Vorne am Hafen etwas Industrie. Ganz normal. Während hinter uns der eisbedeckte Vätnajökull mit den Zähnen knirscht, Trolle durchs Land ziehen, Elfen flüstern und ein Polarhimmel den Atem von Vulkanen zu spüren bekommt.

deserts of sand and rubble before your eyes, as far as the eye can see. The coming winter will bring the next storm surge and more grinding, elemental forces. Keeping a safe distance from the open sea, the orbital route crosses a slate-gray stream on an almost makeshift metal bridge to reach the wide expanse of a river bed. It is hundreds of meters wide, covered with boulders and rubble, crisscrossed with rivulets, streams and small rivers. During the spring melt, gigantic masses of water flow from the mountains to the sea, flooding the entire valley. Wider than any river in Europe, this is just the last evidence of the death-throes of the winter's ice.

Just a few kilometers further on, the road makes its weary way towards the city of Höfn. To the right, huge tufa mountains crumble into rubble, enormous quantities of gray rock roll towards the Icelandic lowlands, ending in a strip of grass and pastureland by the coast. The road now presses through these pastures. We can hardly wait to arrive at our destination, looking forward to the gentle waves of grassland by the sea, which looks a bit like the rural idyll of northern Germany or southern Scandinavia: meadows, small ditches and fences, then the first signs of human habitation, crouching behind rows of trees. A gas station, apartment blocks, then wooden family homes. Gray rectangular shapes. There are some signs of industrial activity at the harbor. Everything looks absolutely normal. And yet, behind us the ice-covered volcano of Vätnajökull grinds its teeth, trolls roam the countryside, elves whisper their secrets and the polar sky is warmed by the breath of volcanoes.

EGILSTAÐIR HÖFN

Eine Welt aus Wasser und Bergen – das sind die Fjorde im Osten Islands. Geformt vom Feuer aus dem Bauch der Erde und dem Gewicht der Eiszeitgletscher strahlt dieses Land eine erhabene und immer wieder auch martialische Urgewalt aus. Die kleine Stadt Seyðisfjörður im gleichnamigen Fjord strahlt eine eigenwillige Ruhe aus, sie ist bis zum Bau des geplanten Tunnels nur im Sommer über den vorgelagerten Gebirgspass zu erreichen. Je weiter man danach an den Fjorden entlang nach Süden fährt, desto beeindruckender wird die Landschaft: In den Himmel ragende Küstengebirge fallen steil zum Meer hin ab, der Nordatlantik brandet gegen einen schwarzen Strand und einen schmalen Streifen Land. Vom Vulkan Vätnajökull streben dann in der Gegend vor Höfn mächtige Geröllflüsse in Richtung Meer, sie sind im Winter eisbedeckt und ähneln im Sommer mit ihren Felsen und Gesteins-Betten den Gebirgsbächen der Alpen – nur ins Hundertfache vergrößert. Eine Landschaft voller Gewalt und Größe eben. In Höfn haben wir dann wieder die Südküste Islands erreicht.

—

The fjords of eastern Iceland are a world of water and mountains. Formed by fire from the bowels of the earth and the weight of Ice Age glaciers, this country exudes a sublime and constantly martial elemental force. The small town of Seyðisfjörður in the fjord of the same name has an idiosyncratic tranquility. Until the planned tunnel is built, it can only be reached in summer over the mountain pass. The further south you drive along the fjords, the more impressive the landscape becomes: sky-high coastal mountains drop steeply towards the sea. The North Atlantic crashes against a dark beach and a narrow strip of land. Mighty rivers of scree flow from the Vätnajökull volcano toward the sea in the area in front of Höfn. These are covered in ice in winter and, with their rocks and stone beds, resemble the mountain streams of the Alps in summer – only a hundred times bigger. This is a landscape full of violence and grandeur. In Höfn we touch the south coast of Iceland once again

350 KM • 6 STUNDEN // 218 MILES • 6 HOURS

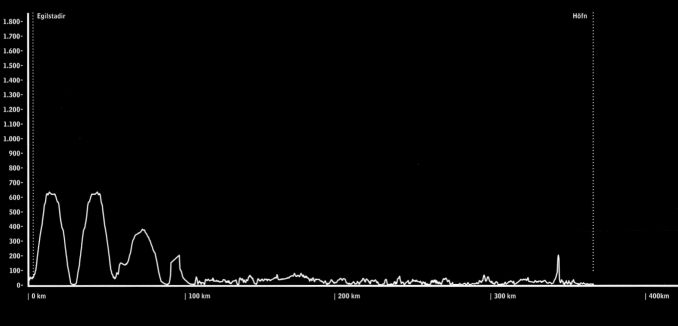

F 985

SUPERTRUCK
4X4 ONLY

HÖFN
GRINDAVIK

580 KM • 10 STUNDEN // 360 MILES • 10 HOURS

Schnurgeradeaus fliegt die Straße dahin, leicht erhaben auf ihrem Fahrbahndamm und ein Schwarm Kurzschnabelgänse folgt ihr. Ein selbstvergessener Pfeil aus Gänse-Pixeln vor dem endlos blassblauen Hintergrund des Polarhimmels. Dann beginnt sich das Asphaltband zu langweilen, schwingt in weitem Bogen nach Süden, hin zum Meer.

—

The road cuts a straight route on a slightly raised embankment. A flock of pink-footed geese follows the same trajectory, like an arrow of goose-shaped pixels against the endless pale blue of the polar sky. The asphalt seems to lose focus, swinging in a wide arc to the south, towards the sea.

F 985

SUPERTRUCK
4X4 ONLY

HOTEL & RESTAURANT

FOSSHOTEL GLACIER LAGOON
HNAPPAVELLIR
785 HNAPPAVELLIR

Die Südküste Islands haben wir bei Höfn weit hinter uns gelassen, in den Wintermonaten ist es so dicht am Atlantik zu unsicher für ein so fragiles Menschen-Bauwerk wie eine Straße. Eis und Schnee packen sich im Land, mit dem beginnenden Frühjahr geben dann Schmelzwasser, Überflutungen und der zermürbende Rhythmus des Auftauens und Einfrierens alles, um die Straße kleinzumachen. Deshalb sucht sie einen sicheren Verlauf im Landesinneren, weit weg vom Fuß der Berge, weit weg vom Gischten des Meeres. Erst viele Kilometer von Höfn entfernt zwingen schroff aufgeschichtete Tafelberge die isländische Ringstraße wieder bis an den Ozean, und dann kommt auch noch der Breiðamerkurjökull daher. Ein eisiger Arm des mächtigen Vatnajökull-Gletschers, der große Flächen des isländischen Südens bedeckt. Früher war der Breiðamerkurjökull angeblich noch bis ans Meer heruntergeschoben, heute geht ihm rund drei Kilometer vor der Küste das Gletscher-Sein aus und er zerfließt zu einer eiskalten, grünblauen Lache, auf der bizarre Eisberge treiben. Jökullsárlón heißt diese über 280 Meter tiefe Lagune, die den letzten Rest der titanenhaften, zermalmenden Energie des Gletschers in alle möglichen Schattierungen von Blau diffundieren lässt.

Die Gletscherlagune wirkt ein wenig wie eine überdimensionierte Theaterkulisse, mit dem haushoch gepackten Eis des Gletschers im Hintergrund, davor eine irisierende, spiegelnde Wasseroberfläche im Sommer und eine türkisblaue Eisfläche im Winter. Die Ringstraße schlottert in dieser Szenerie sozusagen durch den Zuschauerraum, auf einer schmalen Hängebrücke über den Abfluss zum Meer. „Tschuldigung, Tschuldigung", scheint sie verlegen zu raunen, während sie – das Naturschauspiel störend – schüchtern und auf Zehenspitzen durch die Reihen imaginärer Zuschauer schleicht. Wir rollen auf einen der Parkplätze und gehen dann in der Landschaft verloren. Stolpern staunend am Ufer des Gletschersees umher, fragen uns, ob wohl schon jemand auf die Idee gekommen ist, diese Dramatik der Natur als Action-Setting in einem Film zu nutzen, und finden dann, dass das doch

We left the south coast of Iceland far behind us at Höfn. Conditions on the Atlantic seaboard during the winter months are far too treacherous for something as fragile as a coast road. Ice and snow take their toll on the countryside, the alternating thawing and freezing of the spring meltwater cutting the highway down to size, forcing it to seek a safe route inland, far from the mountains and the spray of the sea. We are a long distance from Höfn before craggy table mountains force the Icelandic orbital route to twist back toward the ocean. That's when we encounter the Breiðamerkurjökull, an icy arm of the mighty Vatnajokull Glacier, which covers large areas of the Icelandic south. The story goes that in the past, the Breiðamerkurjökull ran all the way to the sea, but these days it runs out of ice about three kilometers from the coast, melting into an ice-cold, green-blue pool where bizarrely shaped icebergs float. Jökullsárlón is the name of this 280-meter deep lagoon, which allows the last of the titanic, crushing energy of the glacier to diffuse into every imaginable shade of blue.

The glacial lagoon looks a bit like an oversized theater backdrop, with the ice from the glacier packed as high as a house in the background, in front of it an iridescent, reflecting water surface in summer and a turquoise-blue ice surface in winter. The orbital route crosses a narrow suspension bridge over the water as it drains into the sea. It seems almost embarrassed at disrupting the natural spectacle, shyly tiptoeing past rows of imaginary spectators to takes its place for the show. We roll into one of the parking lots and lose ourselves in the landscape. We find ourselves stumbling around in amazement on the shores of the glacial lake, wondering whether someone has already thought of using this place as the setting for an action film. But that would be a little too much... wouldn't it?

In fact we prefer the black lava beach on the other side of Orbital Route 1. The obsidian black sand crunches under our feet. Seeping water turns our footprints into little puddles, resisting the relentless sea breeze. The glacier has broken up into

SUPERTRUCK
4X4 ONLY

SVÍNAFELLSJÖKULL
GLACIER

ein wenig zu dreist wäre. Oder? Und eigentlich mögen wir den schwarzen Lavasand-Strand auf der anderen Seite des Þjóðvegur 1 fast noch lieber. Obsidianschwarz knirscht er unter den Füßen, sammelt sickerndes Wasser in unseren Fußabdrücken und wehrt sich gegen den unbarmherzig daherfegenden Seewind. Der Gletscher hat Eisbrocken in allen Größen bis hierher erbrochen, das Meer die diamantglänzenden Stücke dann entlang der Küste verteilt und zurück auf den Strand geworfen. Wie grob geschliffene Diamanten in einer mit nachtschwarzem Samt ausgeschlagenen Riesen-Schatulle liegen sie nun überall und glänzen, leuchten, blinken. Fremdartig und ätherisch, wunderschön. Weiter vorn am Strand peitscht der Wind weiße Schaumkronen gegen die Küstenlinie, dahinter scheint der Nordatlantik zum offenen Meer hin anzusteigen, graue Wellen schwappen unaufhörlich heran und darunter stürzt sich der Sockel Islands ins Tiefe. – Wie gesagt: Das ist eine grausige, wunderschöne Welt, man steht stumm und ergriffen und etwas furchtsam an dieser Grenze zwischen den Elementen. Liebe Frau Jökullsárlón, seien Sie uns nicht böse: Wir lieben Ihre Majestät und bizarre Schönheit, aber die einfache, herzzerreißende Wildheit des Schwarzen Strands in Ihrer Nachbarschaft hat es uns noch ein Stück mehr angetan.

Am Fuß der riesigen Gletscherfläche des Vatnajökull rollen wir dann lange dahin, schweigend und in uns gekehrt. Jetzt ist gerade nicht der Moment für Smalltalk oder Musik im Autoradio, eine dichte, traumhafte Stimmung hat sich bei uns verfangen. Das Massiv des Öræfajökull leuchtet schneeweiß im Norden und schickt uns lange Gletscher-Arme entgegen, türmt sich zum Himmel empor. Wolken quellen über das Bergmassiv und rasen dann nach Süden, die blassgoldene Sonne scheint in manchen Momenten aus mattem Glas zu sein. – Unterhalb des Skaftafell schlägt die Ringstraße einen weiten Bogen, hier verlassen wir die Hauptstraße für einen Abstecher zu den Wasserfällen der Gegend.

In mit Gestrüpp und Heide bedeckten Hügelkuppen öffnet sich am Ende eines Pfads der Svartifoss, Wasser aus den Bergen strömt hier in ein dunkles Becken, das von Basaltsäulen eingerahmt ist. Wie das verlassene Nest von Aliens sieht es aus, in die Länge gezogene Bienenwaben oder geometrische Orgelpfeifen, die

irregular chunks of ice like diamonds, which the sea throws back onto the beach along the coast. They sparkle and glitter like coarse uncut gemstones nestling in a giant jewelry box lined with midnight velvet, strange, ethereal and beautiful. Further along the beach, the wind whips the waters of the North Atlantic into white caps. The distant open ocean seems to rise up, as gray waves wash back and forth incessantly and Iceland's rock foundations plunge into the marine depths. – As has been observed already, this is a gruesomely beautiful world, where we stand mutely stricken and frightened at this border between the elements. We hope that Jökullsárlón will not take it too much to heart if we admit that, although we love its majesty and bizarre beauty, we are even more attracted to the simple, heartbreaking wildness of the nearby black beach. We continue in inward-looking silence for a while along the foot of the huge glacier area of the Vatnajökull ice cap. Now is not the time for small talk or music on the car radio; a heavy, dreamlike atmosphere has caught up with us.

The snow-white Öræfajökull massif shines to the north, stretching its long glacier arms towards us and reaching towards the sky. Clouds bubble up over the mountain range and then speed their way south. At times the pale golden sun seems to be made of sand-blasted glass. – Below Skaftafell, the orbital road forms a widely curving arc. We leave the main road here for a detour to the nearby waterfalls. Among hilltops covered with scrub and heather, the Svartifoss opens at the end of a trail and water from the mountains flows into a dark basin framed by basalt columns. It looks like an abandoned nest for alien lifeforms, elongated honeycombs or geometric organ pipes that fall toward the water in large blocks. Now, of course, the impressive nature of the Icelandic south has us truly hooked. We drive from one miraculous sight to the next and find ourselves climbing out of the car again and again, following small trails into the wilderness on foot, thunderstruck by dramatic rock formations, strangely lively waterfalls or eternal fields of scree.

The Fjarðarárgljúfur Gorge stamps itself into the black crust of the earth, and moss and undergrowth cling to rugged rock faces like fur. The canyon is like a gaping wound, torn from the earth, not dug into it. Dark water forces a

AROUND KÁLFAFELL

AROUND KÁLFAFELL

FJAÐRÁRGLJÚFUR

an ihrem unteren Ende in großen Blöcken ins Wasser fallen. Jetzt hat uns die beeindruckende Natur des isländischen Südens natürlich erst so richtig am Haken. Wir fahren von Wunder zu Wunder und können gar nicht anders, als immer wieder auszusteigen, kleinen Trails zu Fuß ins Wilde hinein zu folgen und an dramatischen Felsformationen, sonderbar festlichen Wasserfällen oder ewig weiten Geröllfeldern hängen zu bleiben. Unfassbar anderweltig stanzt sich die Fjarðarárgljúfur-Schlucht in die schwarze Erdkruste, Moss und Gestrüpp klammert sich hier wie Fell an schroffe Felswände. Der Canyon klafft offen, ist nicht in den Boden eingegraben, sondern sichtlich durchs Aufreißen der Erde entstanden. Dunkles Wasser drängt sich am Boden der Schlucht dahin, strudelt über Katarakte und sammelt sich für kurze Atempausen in unnatürlich türkisgrünen Becken. Dann geht es geradewegs auf die riesige Kuppe des Myrdalsjökull zu, das Land ähnelt streckenweise eher der Oberfläche des Mondes als einem anderen Ort irgendwo auf der Erde.

Immer weiter fahren wir, vorbei am mächtigen Skógafoss-Wasserfall und in direkter Nachbarschaft des Eyjafjallajökull-Vulkans. Und jetzt zieht es uns ein letztes Mal ins Landesinnere. Bei Hvolsvöllur verlassen wir die Ringstraße und folgen der 2, dem Fljótshilðarvegur, nach Nordosten. Irgendwann endet die Straße und jetzt hast du entweder einen robusten Allrad-Wagen unter dir oder du drehst besser um. Ganz harmlos plätschert die Schotterstraße zuerst dahin, aber ihre Schläge werden härter. Ihr grobes Geröll beginnt zu rutschen und an den Rädern zu saugen, Wasserläufe queren sie, und die sind tiefer als man vermutet hätte. Nach rund 40 Kilometern hat man es auf die Hinterseite des Gebirges im Norden geschafft, kurvt rumpelnd und geprügelt dahin, ringt mit kräftezehrenden Rampen im hügeligen Gelände, befürchtet immer wieder Achsbruch oder gleich völlige Fahrzeugauflösung, während rundum ein verlassenes Land lauert, ob du liegenbleibst. Runde Vulkankegel dringen aus Geröllwüsten, graues Eis kauert zäh im Sonnenschatten der Grate, Millionen Jahre

path along the bottom of the gorge, swirling over cataracts and gathering briefly in unnaturally turquoise-green pools to draw breath. It then heads straight for the mighty summit of Myrdalsjökull, the land in parts looking more like the surface of the moon than any other place on earth. We continue our journey, past the mighty Skógafoss waterfall and closely skirting the Eyjafjallajökull volcano. The route turns inland one last time. At Hvolsvöllur we leave the orbital highway and follow Route 2, the Fljótshilðarvegur, to the north-east. At some point the road comes to an end and now is the time to turn around, unless you have a sturdy four-wheel drive vehicle. The gravel road is harmless enough at first, but soon starts to get more difficult. The coarse shale begins to slide and pull on the wheels. Water crosses your path, deeper than expected. After about 40 kilometers you make it to the other side of the mountains in the north, not quite beaten into submission and gamely wrestling with exhausting slopes on the hilly terrain. You live in constant fear that you will break an axle or that your car will completely disintegrate. All around you a desert landscape waits for you to break down. Volcanic cones emerge from fields of rubble, gray ice tenaciously grips the shaded ridges. Millions of years of erosion ceaselessly and mercilessly pulverize all in their path – not just the stone, but you too.

If you had one of Iceland's familiar all-terrain vehicles, you might make it to Landmannalaugur near the 1490-meter high Hekla volcano. The best choice would be an Arctic truck on huge balloon tires with long spring deflection travel or at least a really tough off-road vehicle. You start to run into problems as soon as the land is tougher than your vehicle and that precisely what you don't want here. After all, you not only want to make it there, but also back again. We're taking the long way over the Tindfjallajökull, past Ymir and Yma, back to the orbital route east of the Þjórsá river. The highway seems strangely peaceful and reassuring now and we find this hint of civilization, incredibly calming. At Selfoss we cross the Ólfusá, driving to Hveragerði, where we receive confirmation

HOTEL & RESTAURANT

HÓTEL KRÍA
SLÉTTUVEGUR 12-14
870 VÍK Í MÝRDAL
WWW.HOTELKRIA.IS

RESTAURANT SUDUR-VÍK
SUDURVEGUR 1 870, VÍK

VIK

REYNISDRANGAR

DYRHÓLAEY

SÓLHEIMAJÖKULSVEGUR

MAELIFELL

SUPERTRUCK
4X4 ONLY

AROUND
LANDMANNALAUGAR

SUPERTRUCK
4X4 ONLY

Erosion pulverisieren unaufhörlich und lieblos jede Materie. Nicht nur den Stein. Auch. Dich.

Bis zum Landmannalaugur im Einzugsbereich des 1.490 Meter hohen Hekla-Vulkan könntest du es schaffen – wie gesagt, falls du eines der Maschinengewächse Islands unter dir hast. Am besten einen Arctic-Truck auf kindergroßen Ballon-Reifen und mit ellenlangen Federwegen oder wenigstens einen wirklich harten Geländewagen. Sobald das Land härter ist als deine Maschine, hast du ein Problem. Und das willst du hier nicht haben. Weil du es ja nicht nur bis hierhin schaffen willst, sondern auch zurück. Den langen Weg über den Tindfjallajökull, vorbei an Ymir und Yma, bis zurück zur Ringstraße östlich des Þjórsá-Flusses. Die kommt einem jetzt sonderbar friedlich und zuversichtlich vor. Zivilisation pur, unfassbar beruhigend. Bei Selfoss überqueren wir den Ólfusá, fahren bis Hveragerði und hier bewahrheitet sich unser plötzlicher Eindruck aus einer knirschenden Vulkanreise zurück in der unbekümmerten, leichtlebigen Welt der Menschen zu sein. In Glashäusern beheizt mit Geothermie wachsen hier Islands beste Tomaten – und wenn Isländer sagen „Islands Beste", meinen sie natürlich: die besten der Welt. Angeber waren die Wikinger noch nie, aber eine klare Ansage zwischen den Zeilen machen können sie durchaus. Besser als irgendjemand sonst auf der Welt. Ach was: im Universum.

Unsere Stimmung ist gelöst. Anstatt geradewegs zurück nach Reykjavík zu fahren, rollen wir am Meer entlang: Ölfus, Grindavík, dann ums südliche Kap Islands herum bis Hafnir, an Reykjanesbær vorbei und jetzt – erst jetzt – haben wir Island umrundet. Das Ende der Reise ist ihr Anfang. Dies, und nur dies, hat Island mit allen anderen Inseln der Welt gemeinsam. Repeat, Rewind. Wir werden wiederkommen.

Den langen Weg über den Tindfjallajökull, vorbei an Ymir und Yma, bis zurück zur Ringstraße östlich des Þjórsá-Flusses. Die kommt einem jetzt sonderbar friedlich und zuversichtlich vor. Zivilisation pur, unfassbar beruhigend. Bei Selfoss überqueren wir den Ólfusá, fahren bis Hveragerði und hier bewahrheitet sich unser plötzlicher Eindruck aus einer knirschenden Vulkanreise zurück in der unbekümmerten, leichtlebigen Welt der Menschen zu sein.

We're taking the long way over the Tindfjallajökull, past Ymir and Yma, back to the orbital route east of the Þjórsá river. The highway seems strangely peaceful and reassuring now and we find this hint of civilization, incredibly calming. At Selfoss we cross the Ólfusá, driving to Hveragerði, where we receive confirmation that we have made it back from our bone-crunching volcanic journey to the carefree, easy-going world of men.

that we have made it back from our bone-crunching volcanic journey to the carefree, easy-going world of men. Iceland's best tomatoes grow here in greenhouses heated by geothermal energy.

When Icelanders say "the best in Iceland", they naturally mean the best in the world. The Vikings were never boastful people, but it's not hard to read between the lines when they make a clear statement. Better than anyone else in the world. Or the universe for that matter. Our mood relaxes and instead of making our way straight back to Reykjavík, we take a spin along the coast: Ölfus, Grindavík, then around the southern Cape of Iceland to Hafnir, past Reykjanesbær and now – only now – we have completed the circuit of Iceland.

The end of the journey is also its beginning. This is perhaps the only thing Iceland has in common with all other islands of the world. Repeat, rewind. We'll be back.

RESTAURANT

CAFÉ BRYGGJAN
MIDGARDUR 2
GRINDAVIK

**AROUND
LANDMANNALAUGAR**

SUPERTRUCK
4X4 ONLY

SUPERTRUCK
4X4 ONLY

KLEIFARVATN

AROUND GRINDAVIK

HÖFN GRINDAVIK

Nach einem Start in Höfn, einer der größeren Städte an der Südküste Islands, führt uns die letzte Etappe direkt am Fuß der riesigen Vulkanmassive des Vatnajökull und Myrdalsjökull entlang. Bis auf wenige Gehöfte und kleinere Ansiedlungen ist die Gegend über viele Kilometer hinweg menschenleer, allerdings ziehen Natur und Landschaft zu den meisten Jahreszeiten viele Besucher an. Die Natur ist geprägt von vielfältigen Schauspielen und eigentümlicher Faszination, Island zeigt wieder einmal sein vulkanisches Gesicht. Die Dramatik dieser Landschaft inspiriert Filmemacher und Fotografen aus der ganzen Welt, so kennt man zum Beispiel die Jökulsárlón-Lagune aus James-Bond-Filmen oder Werbespots. Immer wieder übernimmt die Natur auch selbst Regie, wird zum Hauptdarsteller und zum Drehbuchschreiber. So ist vor allem der Vulkanausbruch des Eyjafjallajökull Ende März 2010 wohldokumentiert, als über Tage hinweg der Flugverkehr über dem Nordatlantik durch in die Atmosphäre geschleuderte Aschewolken zum Erliegen kam. Bei einem Besuch des Landesinneren wechseln wir auf robustes und geländegängiges Gerät und schaffen es so bis zum Vulkan Hekla und an die heißen Quellen von Landmannalaugur. Südlich von Reykjavík kommen wir wieder in dichter besiedelte Gegenden, ein letzter Bogen um die südwestliche Landzunge Islands führt uns zurück in die Hauptstadt und an den Beginn unserer Reise.

—

Starting in Höfn, one of the larger towns on the south coast of Iceland, the last stage takes us right to the foot of the huge volcanic massifs of Vatnajökull and Myrdalsjökull. With the exception of a few farmsteads and smaller settlements, the area is deserted for miles, although nature and the landscape attract numerous visitors at most times of the year. Iceland's natural beauty is shaped by diverse spectacles and exerts a peculiar fascination. The island's volcanic face is there for all to see. The drama of this landscape has inspired filmmakers and photographers from all over the world. For example the Jökulsárlón lagoon is familiar from James Bond movies and commercials. Again and again, nature itself takes over as director, leading actor and scriptwriter. In particular, people will remember the volcanic eruption of Eyjafjallajökull at the end of March 2010, when air traffic over the North Atlantic came to a standstill for days due to ash clouds thrown into the atmosphere. When exploring the interior of the country, we switch to a robust, all-terrain vehicle that takes us to the Hekla volcano and the hot springs of Landmannalaugur. South of Reykjavík we find ourselves back in more densely populated areas, completing one last arc around Iceland's southwestern headland, which leads us back to the capital and to where our journey began.

580 KM • 10 STUNDEN // 360 MILES • 10 HOURS

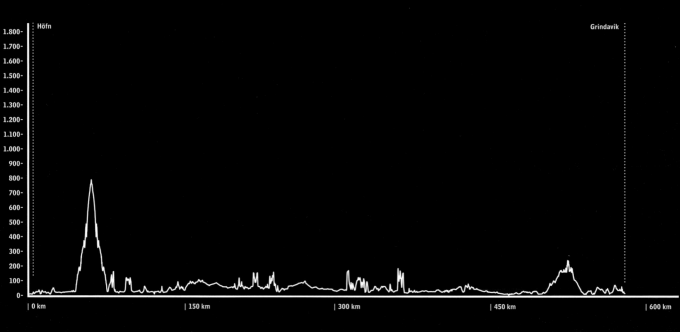

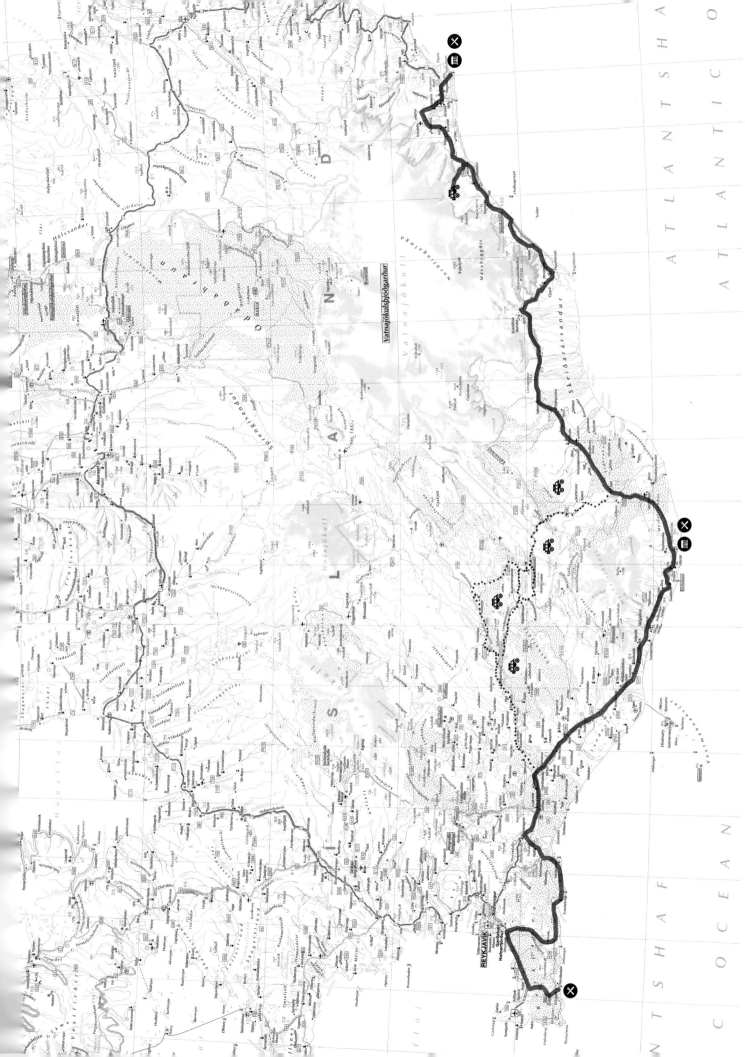

WORTH A VISIT: ICELAND´S MUSEUMS

AKUREYRI ART MUSEUM
YSTAFELL TRANSPORTATION MUSEUM
WESTFJORD HISTORY MUSEUM, ÍSAFJÖRÐUR
THE HERRING ERA MUSEUM, SIGLUFJÖRÐUR
FACTORY CAR MUSEUM, BREIÐDALSVÍK
REYKJAVÍK´S ART MUSEUM

Islands Besonderheit sind die Museen. Beinahe jedes Dorf scheint eins zu haben, teilweise finden sich sogar private Minimuseen in abgelegenen Gegenden, und die Themenvielfalt ist immens. Dass die Hauptstadt Reykjavík mit vielen Museen glänzt, dürfte noch nicht besonders überraschen, dass aber selbst ein kleines Fischerstädtchen wie Húsavik im Norden Islands mit gleich drei Museen – von obskur bis spannend – aufwartet, kann schon verblüffen: Wir staunen uns durchs Entdecker-Museum, wundern uns im Safnahúsið-Museum der regionalen Besonderheiten über genau die und bekommen auch im Wal-Museum kaum den Mund wieder zu. Technik-Fans macht das Luftfahrt- und Motorradmuseum in Akureyri glücklich – die übers ganze Land verteilten, großartigen und überraschenden Automuseen haben wir damit allerdings nicht einmal erwähnt.

Das Icelandic Wartime Museum in Fjardabyggd macht nachdenklich, das „French Museum" von Fáskrúðsfjörður ist ganz besonders, das Maritime Museum von Ísafjörður ebenso voller atlantischer Wunder wie das Heringmuseum in Siglufjörður. Die „Viking World" in Keflavik macht auf unerwartet modern, die Höhlenhäuser von Laugarvatn auf nostalgisch. Und wie gesagt: Das wäre jetzt nur eine ganz kleine Auswahl.

Iceland's specialises in museums. Almost every village seems to have one. In some cases there are even tiny private museums in remote locations. The variety of topics covered is immense. It's probably not that suprising that the capital Reykjavík has so many museums, but the fact that even a small fishing colony like Húsavik in northern Iceland has three museums, ranging from the obscure to the awe-inspiring: we find the Museum of Exploration surprising, the Safnahúsið-Museum of Regional Curiosities intriguing and the Whale Museum simply astonishing.

Technology enthusiasts will be happy at the Aviation and Motorcycle Museum in Akureyri, not to mention the wonderful and surprising motor museums scattered all over the country.

The Icelandic Wartime Museum in Fjardabyggd is thought-provoking, the "French Museum" of Fáskrúðsfjörður is something very special indeed, while the Maritime Museum of Ísafjörður is as full of Atlantic wonders as the Herring Museum in Siglufjörður. The "Viking World" in Keflavik makes an unexpectedly modern impression, while the cave dwellings of Laugarvatn seem nostalgic. And remember: that's just a very small selection.

ASK THE LOCALS

Auf Island wohnen und Porsche fahren – das ist schon mal keine so offensichtliche Kombination. Was sind das für Typen, die einem da begegnen? Zunächst mal raue Kerle. Echte Nordmänner. Mit ganz harter Schale. Dann lernst du sie kennen, und sie sind unglaublich nett, mit ganz weichem Kern. So wie Björki zum Beispiel. Der repariert in seiner Werkstatt knüppelharte Arctic Trucks – aber auch Porsches. Oder Petur, der den Porsche Club Island leitet und dich gern vom Flughafen abholt. Allerdings nicht in Reykjavík, sondern bei dir zu Hause, in München, mit der 757, die er normalerweise für Icelandair pilotiert. Und schließlich Fusi, für den das Motto „geht nicht, gibt's nicht" erfunden wurde, denn er kennt wirklich jeden. Wirklich. Jeden. Wenn er nicht in Island ist, lebt er in Florida. Mehr Kontrast geht auch nicht. Wie das Land, so die Leute.

–

Living in Iceland and driving a Porsche is not the most obvious of combinations. What kind of people can you expect you meet there? At first impression they seem like real roustabouts. Typical northerners: genuine tough nuts. Then you get to know them and find they are incredibly decent, soft-hearted guys. Take Björki, for example. He repairs rough, tough Arctic trucks in his workshop – as well as Porsches. Or Petur, who runs the Porsche Club Iceland and is happy to pick you up at the airport. Not in Reykjavík, however, but at your home, in Munich, in the 757 he normally pilots for Icelandair. And finally Fusi, for whom the word "impossible" simply does not exist, because he genuinely seems to know everyone. And I mean everyone. When he's not in Iceland, he lives in Florida. You can't get a bigger contrast than that. You could say that the country is just like the people.

Gibt es Elfen wirklich? *Björki:* Natürlich, kein Zweifel. *Petur:* Nein, aber das ist eine schöne Geschichte für die Kinder. *Fusi:* Ja, natürlich gibt es Elfen. – Ich habe es selbst erlebt!

Was ist die Essenz von Island? *Björki:* KRAFT. Wenn man die Wasserfälle, Vulkane und das Wetter kombiniert, erhält man rohe Kraft. *Petur:* Reine Natur und freundliche Menschen. *Fusi:* Natürliche Schönheit, saubere Luft und Wasser.

Allradantrieb oder Hinterradantrieb? *Björki:* Ist das eine echte Frage? Hinterradantrieb ist die beste Wahl! *Petur:* Allradantrieb im Winter und Zweiradantrieb im Sommer :-) *Fusi:* Hinterradantrieb beim Porsche, aber Allradantrieb beim Truck.

Jahresdurchschnittstemperatur um den Gefrierpunkt, Winter von Oktober bis April … – Warum fährst du als Isländer immer noch einen Porsche? *Björki:* Bei einem Porsche geht es nicht nur ums Fahren. Es geht um so viele andere Dinge. Zum Beispiel um die Möglichkeit, das Auto in der heimischen Garage zu haben. Manchmal fahre ich dorthin, um mir das Auto anzusehen, was für ein Kunstwerk! *Petur:* Porsche ist immer die erste Wahl für alle Jahreszeiten. *Fusi:* Porsche fahren kann man im Winter genauso gut wie im Sommer – ich montiere einfach einen Satz Winterreifen.

Was ist deine Hausstrecke und warum? *Björki:* Die ist immer gleich. Ich wohne in der Nähe der Arbeit und bin normalerweise schneller zu Hause, als ich denken kann. Aber nach einem stressigen Tag gibt es nichts Schöneres, als eine lange Strecke in einem guten Auto zu fahren. Sobald man zu Hause ist, sind alle Sorgen weg. *Petur:* Zum Flughafen und zurück, zum Arbeitsplatz. *Fusi:* Flottamannaleið. Eine schöne Strecke, die von Hafnarfjörður nach Reykjavík führt, und zwar von hinten!

Was ist dein Soundtrack beim Fahren? *Björki:* Es klingt vielleicht nach Klischee, aber das ist „Born to be Wild". Ich finde, das ist der ultimative Soundtrack zum Autofahren. *Petur:* 80er-Jahre-Musik. *Fusi:* Derzeit Dua Lipa und „Future Nostalgia".

Ich bin nur für einen Tag in Island. – Was muss ich unbedingt machen? *Björki:* Du solltest den Suðurstrandavegur fahren. Das ist eine der besten Straßen des Landes. Und wenn dir das nicht reicht und du Zeit hast, kannst du den derzeit aktiven Vulkan besuchen, der nur wenige Gehminuten von der Straße entfernt ist. *Petur:* Einfach irgendwohin fahren, mit einem Porsche. *Fusi:* Ein Tag in Island ist nicht genug! Aber wenn man bei Sonnenaufgang am Thingvellir-See aufwacht und die Schönheit der Gegend zusammen mit den ersten Sonnenstrahlen auf sich wirken

Do elves really exist? *Björki:* Of course they do, without a doubt. *Petur:* No, but it's a nice story for the kids. *Fusi:* Yes, of course they do. – I've had first-hand experience!

What is the essence of Iceland? *Björki:* POWER. The combination of waterfalls, volcanos and weather conditions results in raw power. *Petur:* Natural beauty, clean air and water. *Fusi:* Natural beauty, clean air and water.

All-wheel drive or rear-wheel drive? *Björki:* Are you for real? Rear wheel drive rules! *Petur:* All-wheel drive in winter and two-wheel drive in summer :-) *Fusi:* I'll take a rear-wheel drive Porsche, but a four-wheel drive truck.

Average annual temperature around freezing point, winter from October to April… - why do you, as an Icelander, still drive a Porsche? *Björki:* Having a Porsche is not just about driving. It is about so many other things. One of them being the chance to have your car at home in your garage. Sometimes I just go there to admire the car, what a piece of art! *Petur:* Porsche is always the first choice for all seasons. *Fusi:* Porsches perform just as well in winter as they do in the summertime – I just fit a set of winter tires.

What is your home route and why? *Björki:* It's always the same. I live close to work and I'm usually home before I know it. However, after a stressful day, there's nothing better than taking the long way in a great car. Once you've arrived home, all your worries are gone. *Petur:* To the airport and back for work. *Fusi:* Flottamannaleið. A lovely route that takes you from Hafnarfjörður to Reykjavík from the back!

What is your driving soundtrack? *Björki:* This may sound like a cliché but it's "Born to be Wild". For me it's the ultimate driving soundtrack. *Petur:* 80's music. *Fusi:* Currently Dua Lipa and "Future Nostalgia".

Let's imagine I have just one day to spend in Iceland. – What should I do…? *Björki:* You should drive the south coast road (Suðurstrandavegur). It's one of the best roads for driving in the country. If that's not enough and you have the time, you could stop by the currently active volcano within walking distance from the road. *Petur:* Just go anywhere for a drive in a Porsche. *Fusi:* COne day in Iceland is not enough! But if you wake up at Lake Thingvellir at sunrise and take in the beauty of the surroundings in the first rays of the sun, you are off to a great start. Plus you have your choice of great driving roads. Have a bowl of tomato soup in Fridheimar. Explore the great waterfalls of the south and take an ice cold shower in Gljúfrabúi. Make you way back to Reykjavík along the south coast with its black sand beaches, preferably driving

Du solltest den Suðurstrandavegur fahren. Das ist eine der besten Straßen des Landes. Und wenn dir das nicht reicht und du Zeit hast, kannst du den derzeit aktiven Vulkan besuchen, der nur wenige Gehminuten von der Straße entfernt ist.

You should drive the south coast road (Suðurstrandavegur). It's one of the best roads for driving in the country. If that's not enough and you have the time, you could stop by the currently active volcano within walking distance from the road.

lässt, hat man einen tollen Start. Außerdem bist du von tollen Strecken umgeben. Iss eine Tomatensuppe in Fridheimar. Erkunde die großen Wasserfälle des Südens und erlebe die eiskalte Dusche in Gljúfrabúi. Fahr entlang der Südküste mit ihren schwarzen Sandstränden zurück nach Reykjavík, am besten vorbei an den heißen Quellen von Krísuvík und dem unwirklichen See Kleifarvatn, ebenfalls eine tolle Strecke. Dann ein schnelles Abendessen im Fish and Chips Vagninn unten am Hafen. Beenden kann man den Tag mit einem Bad im beruhigenden Wasser der Sky Lagoon, da genießt du den Sonnenuntergang und – je nach Jahreszeit – sogar das Nordlicht!

Was unterscheidet die Porsche-Szene in Island von der im Rest der Welt - oder ist Porsche Liebe einfach nur Porsche Liebe? *Björki:* Ich glaube, die Marke ist der Klebstoff, der alles zusammenhält. Davon abgesehen meine ich, dass die Porsche-Szene in Island einzigartig ist. Man kennt fast jeden mit Namen, man weiß, wer welches Auto besitzt, und viele von ihnen sind gute Freunde von mir. *Petur:* Manchmal ist es schwierig, im Winter zu fahren, aber im Allgemeinen ist es ein riesiges Vergnügen und die Liebe ist groß. *Fusi:* Die verrückten Isländer sind das eine, aber die Begeisterung für die Marke Porsche ist universell. Trotzdem ist unsere Saison für klassische Porsches eigentlich zu kurz – in einem guten Jahr sind es nur vier Monate ...

past the hot springs of Krísuvík and otherworldly Lake Kleifarvatn, which is also a fun road to drive. Have a quick bite to eat at The Fish and Chips Vagninn down by the harbor. Then end the day by soaking in the serene waters of the Sky Lagoon, enjoying the sunset and even the northern lights, depending on the time of year!

What makes the Porsche scene in Iceland different from that in the rest of the world - or is Porsche love just Porsche love wherever you are? *Björki:* I think the brand is the glue that holds everything together. That being said, I think the Porsche scene in Iceland is quite unique. You know almost everybody by name, you know what cars they own and many of them are good friends of mine. *Petur:* Sometimes it can be hard to drive in the winter, but generally it's a real pleasure and you can feel the love. *Fusi:* Crazy Icelanders for one thing, but enthusiasm for the Porsche brand is universal. Still, our season for classic Porsches is too short – even in a good year it only lasts four months...

BAC KST AGE

Alle Speicher leer. Das ist oft unsere Statusanzeige, bevor wir die wunderbare Porsche-Community Islands besuchen. Wir kennen die Freunde dort oben schon eine ganze Weile: Fusi den Netzwerker und Björki in seiner Garage oder Petur, der entweder eine Boeing 757 für Iceland Air fliegt oder den Porsche Club Island steuert. Und nach ein paar Tagen Island sind die Akkus der Seele dann wieder voll, die Insel ist eine Ladestation. Von abgewetzt und ausgepowert auf hellwach, tiefenentspannt und ON. Nach mittlerweile sechs Begegnungen mit Island zu allen Jahreszeiten wollen wir uns deshalb mit dieser CURVES-Ausgabe revanchieren. Den Hut vor diesem Wunderland am Polarkreis ziehen, seine Geschichte erzählen und die CURVES-Leser mit auf eine Reise rund um die Insel nehmen. Es wurde Zeit.

Island hat uns dabei wieder einmal überrascht. Man kann es nicht anders sagen: Was Sie in den Händen halten, ist die Spitze eines Eisbergs. Der Kegel des Vulkans. Island sprengt Objektive, lässt Kamerasensoren glühen,

Running on empty is a feeling we often experience before visiting Iceland's wonderful Porsche community. We've had friends up there going back a long time: Fusi the network specialist, Björki in his garage and Petur, who divides his time between flying a Boeing 757 for Iceland Air and running Porsche Club Iceland. After just a few days in Iceland our batteries have been replenished, as the island acts like a charging station. We have switched from worn out and exhausted to wide awake, deeply relaxed and ready for anything. After six visits to Iceland at different times of year, we want to return the favor with this issue of CURVES. We salute this miraculous country in the Arctic Circle, telling its story and taking our CURVES readers on a journey around the island. It was about time.

Yet again, Iceland managed to spring a few surprises. There is no other way to describe it: what you are holding here in your hands is just the tip of the iceberg or, more aptly, the cone of the volcano. Iceland is almost impossible to capture on camera, sending sensors into

sorgt für eine unfassbare Flut der Bilder. Vielleicht ist der eigentlich beeindruckende Moment dieser Reise also genau jetzt erreicht: Beim Sichten des entstandenen Bildmaterials, Auge in Auge mit den fest eingebrannten Erinnerungen an viele Hunderte Kilometer. An das Wetter, den Wind, die Menschen, die Straße. Deshalb mögen wir die stillen Stunden am Bildschirm auch so, zu Hause im CURVES-Büro, wenn das ferne Land im Dunst verschwunden ist und durch die Bilder und Filme zurückkehrt. Wenn aus den Einhundertstel-Momentaufnahmen eine Geschichte werden soll, die unsere Leser abholt und mitnimmt. Wir haben bei jeder CURVES-Ausgabe seit mittlerweile 10 Jahren selbst gestaunt, was sich da so alles unter dem Auge der Kamera gezeigt hat. Dinge, die wir vielleicht im Moment des Erlebens und Fotografierens oder Filmens überhaupt nicht bemerkt hatten. Plötzlich sind sie da: Strukturen, Farben, große Wildheit, kleine Schönheit. Wie gesagt – wir entdecken das seit 10 Jahren immer wieder. Island bläst uns in dieser Hinsicht jedoch vollkommen weg. Dass wir dort waren – unter den lavaspeienden Vulkanen, am grau mahlenden Meer des Nordens, in den weiten Monochrom-Schotterwüsten und Multicolor-Landschaften – das berührt uns selbst. Und wir beginnen uns Fragen zu stellen: Wie war das noch? Was wäre gewesen, wenn? Nur einen Tag früher oder später – und dann?

Sagen wir es so: Die CURVES-Leser sollten sich nicht über einen zukünftigen zweiten oder dritten Band dieser Reise wundern. Material genug haben wir. Keine Sekunde Langweile. Aber vielleicht werden wir es auch anders machen. Und in ein paar Monaten zurück nach Island gehen, zu dieser kleinen Schotterstraße, an der wir vor ein paar Tagen umgekehrt sind. Die auf diesem einen Foto und in dieser einen Erinnerung aber immer noch fragt: „Willst du nicht wissen, was an meinem Ende ist?"

Zugegeben, die Schotterstraße ins menschenleere Landesinnere zieht uns auch deshalb magisch an, weil wir Blut geleckt haben, wenn es um Arctic Trucks geht. Um diese hochgelegten All-Terrain-Monster auf ihren massigen Reifen, die über fußballgroße Felsbrocken preschen, ohne zu zucken. Die durch hüfttiefes Wasser waten, steile Schotterrampen hinaufpflügen und selbst auf tiefem Schnee unablässig voranschieben. Beinahe hätten wir auf Island deshalb die CURVES vergessen und diese Ausgabe STONES genannt, denn davon gibt es auf Island viele: Steine. In allen Farben und Größen. Von den obsidianschwarzen Sandkörnern an den Stränden im Süden, die im Meereswind grieseln oder in schimmernden Eisklumpen eingefroren sind, als anorganische 100.000 Jahre alte Gesteinsfliegen

meltdown, while still ensuring an incredible flood of images. Perhaps we have reached the most impressive moment of this journey: while looking through the resulting pictorial record, we come face to face with the indelible memories of many hundreds of kilometers traveled: the weather, the wind, the people, the road. This is the reason why we have enjoyed spending some quiet time revisiting the images in the comfort of the CURVES office. Although the country has disappeared in a distant haze, it comes back with a bang in the photos and videos. Even just a small percentage of the snapshots taken are more than enough to make an engrossing story for our readers, taking them on the journey with us. In every issue of CURVES produced over the last 10 years we have been amazed at what the camera has captured; things that we might missed entirely in the heat of the moment while photographing or filming. Suddenly they are there: structures, colors, wildness, tiny beauties. To repeat: this is something we have discovered again and again over a period of 10 years. But Iceland blows us away completely in this regard. It's hard to believe that we were actually there, in the shadow of lava-spewing volcanoes, on the grinding gray North Atlantic coast, crossing vast monochrome deserts and multicolored landscapes. We start to ask ourselves: Was it actually the way we remember? What might have been? What if we arrived just a day earlier or later?

Let's put it this way: CURVES readers shouldn't be surprised to find us publishing a second or third issue on this journey at some stage in the future. We have more than enough material to ensure not a moment's boredom. Maybe we'll do things differently and return to Iceland in a few months' time. We may need to go back to the little gravel road where we turned back just a few days ago. The photo revisits a question that still lingers in the memory: "Aren't you curious to know what lies at the end?" Admittedly, the gravel road into the deserted interior of the country also attracts us as if by magic. After all, we have acquired an appreciation for the Arctic trucks that enabled us to plow through waist-deep water, climb steep gravel inclines and press forward undaunted, even in deep snow. These high-riding all-terrain monsters have massive tires that can negotiate football-sized boulders with ease. Iceland's vast, rocky landscape is one of the reasons why we were tempted to call this issue STONES instead of CURVES. These stones come in all shapes and sizes: from the obsidian-black grains of sand on the beaches of the south, scattered far and wide by the wind or frozen in shimmering lumps of ice, to the

in den eiskalten, glasklaren Bernstein-Tränen der Gletscher. Über die grobporigen Tuffbrocken, die unaufhörlich in den Becken der Wasserfälle rumpeln, und wenn man sie herausholt, tropfen sie einen Moment lang, saugen dann den letzten Rest von Wasser in sich hinein und werden schließlich matt, taub, hautfräsend. Bis hin zu den Felsen, die sich von den Wänden der Plateauberge werfen, als kantige Trümmer der Erosion, und dabei brüllen: Steine sind anders als Menschen, die größten unter ihnen sind die jüngsten und die Stein-Greise sind Sand. Man kann das kaum anders sagen, denn die Majestät und der Zauber Islands lassen einen das Besondere hinter allen Dingen sehen – aber wir wollen nicht ablenken. Islands Schönheit hat schließlich einen festen Händedruck. Die Insel macht es einem nicht leicht. Sie ist groß und rau und schonungslos. Wir sind deshalb froh, den langen Weg um die Insel in zwei Fahrzeugen gemacht zu haben, die unterschiedlicher nicht sein könnten und dennoch eine gemeinsame Schnittmenge haben: Sie wissen, wie man einen festen Händeruck erwidert. Jung und alt, Old School und New Kid on the Block, Porsche Cayenne Turbo Serie 1 und Porsche Taycan Cross Turismo.

Die Beharrlichkeit und Wildheit und Gelassenheit, mit der uns der gereifte Cayenne während so vieler Kilometer über die Insel bewegt hat, haben uns immer wieder staunen lassen. Was für ein Haudegen. Und gerade als wir uns an den großen, alten Kämpen so richtig gewöhnt hatten, kam für die letzte Etappe der Taycan Cross Turismo ins Spiel, weil da diese Theorie im Raum stand: In einem Land, das Strom aus Wind und Wasser zieht, sich mit Geothermie wärmt und ernährt, müsste ein Elektroauto doch irgendwie sehr überzeugend sein. Wir kennen den Porsche Taycan bereits, er ist eine Offenbarung: schnell, still, atmosphärisch dicht, wunderbar. Die bärenstarke Cross-Turismo-Variante, dieses schotterfetzende Allrad-Gerät, das wikingerstark und nordisch-pur dahinstürmt, hat uns allerdings wirklich mitgerissen. Wir sagen Danke an Porsche und Porsche Island für die Leihgabe dieses großartigen Fahrzeugs – und für die tatkräftige und nachhaltige Unterstützung seit vielen tausend CURVES-Kilometern. Diese Großzügigkeit hält unsere Drehzahlmessernadel oben, diese Großzügigkeit lässt uns Geschichten über eine Welt erzählen, die allen gehört. Auch wenn sich Fahrradfahrer und Motorradfahrer beim Nachfahren der Island-Etappen definitiv warm anziehen müssen, so viel sei verraten ...

Danke auch an Island. An die Freunde. Und an die Menschen, die wir so ungemein freundlich, positiv und unterstützend erlebt haben. Die dünne Schicht aus höflichem Desinteresse weicht nach wenigen Worten ebenso gelassener wie hartnäckiger Hilfsbereitschaft und einer eisgekühlten Fröhlichkeit, die kracht und knarrt wie die Eisschollen im Meer des Nordatlantiks. Man hat uns auf Vulkane geholfen und in die Hinter- und Wohnzimmer gelassen – Island ist so schön, weil die Leute so besonders sind. Wir sagen: Takk!

100,000-year-old insects trapped in the ice-cold, crystal-clear amber tears of the glaciers. From the coarse chunks of tufa that churn endlessly at the base of the waterfalls, becoming dull, numb and abrasive when removed from the water, to the rocks that fling themselves from the flat-topped mountains with a corrosive roar. Stones are very different from people, the largest of them are the youngest while the oldest are tiny grains of sand.

It is almost impossible to express yourself in any other way, because the majesty and the magic of Iceland encourage you to see what it is that makes everything special. But let's not get distracted. Iceland's beauty is something that holds you tight. The island doesn't release its grip easily. It is vast, raw and merciless. That's why we're glad to have made the long trip around the island in two vehicles that couldn't be more different and yet have something in common: they know the secret of a firm grip. Young and old, old school and new kid on the block, the Porsche Cayenne Turbo Series 1 and the Porsche Taycan Cross Turismo.

We have been amazed over and over again by the stamina, wildness of heart and serenity that the venerable Cayenne has demonstrated in taking us around the island. What a trooper! Just as we were getting used to the big, old campaigner, the Taycan Cross Turismo was taken out of the toy box for the last stage. Someone had come up with the theory that an electric car would be just the ticket in a country that produces electricity from wind and water, as well as heat and nourishment from geothermal energy. Although we are already familiar with the Porsche Taycan, it proves to be a revelation: fast, quiet, hermetically sealed – simply wonderful. We've been bowled over by the powerful Cross-Turismo variant, a gravel-chewing all-wheel drive model that storms the roads with the authentic Nordic fury of a modern-day Viking. We'd like to thank Porsche and Porsche Iceland for lending us this great vehicle and for the active and sustained support shown over the many thousands of kilometers covered for CURVES. This generosity of spirit helps keep us going, enabling us to tell stories of a world that belongs to us all, although cyclists and bikers will admittedly need to dress more warmly to complete the various stages of the Icelandic journey described here...

We should remember to thank Iceland itself. Thanks also to all our friends. And to the local people, whom we have found to be extremely friendly, positive and supportive. After a few words, the thin layer of polite reserve gives way to relaxed and dogged helpfulness and a frost-bitten cheeriness that cracks and creaks like the ice floes in the North Atlantic. We were helped up the sides of volcanoes and let into people's living rooms and kitchens – Iceland is so beautiful because its people are so special. We'd like to say: Takk!

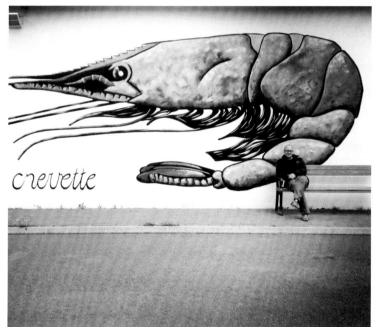

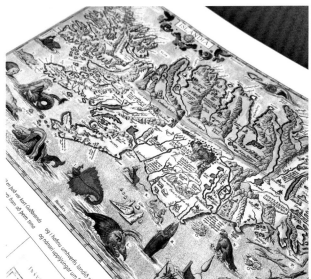

DANK AN / THANKS TO
Bastian Schramm, Maximilian Ramisch, Ben Winter, Nadja Kneissler, Axel Gerber, Hanno Vienken, Michael Dorn, Michael Daiminger, Michaela Bogner

SPECIAL FX / SPECIAL FX
Pétur L. Lentz, Sigfus B Sverrisson for their help and friendship
Porsche umboðið á Íslandi: Benedikt Eyjólfsson, Stálsmiðjan *(For letting us use the Ship Yard location)*, HS Orka *for use of their facilities at The Svartsengi Power Plant)*
Hallgrímur Smári Þorvaldsson, Þorgrímur St Árnason, ORF Genetics – Bio Effect *(for their location in Grindavik)*, Berglind Johansen - Factory Car Museum
Ingólfur Finnbogason, Ólafur Hvanndal, Ingólfur Finnsson, Guðbjartur Guðmundsson
Snæbjörn Jónsson *(Cessna pilot)*

CURVES TRAVEL AGENT:
AOT Travel • info@aottravel.de • Tel. +49 89 12 24 800

COPYRIGHT: Das Werk einschließlich aller seiner Teile ist urheberrechtlich geschützt. Jede Verwertung außerhalb der engen Grenzen des Urheberrechtsgesetzes bedarf der Zustimmung des Urhebers und des Verlags. Die im Inhalt genannten Personen und Handlungen sind frei erfunden. Sollten Ähnlichkeiten mit tatsächlich existenten Personen oder stattgefundenen Handlungen entstanden sein, oder sollte ein solcher Eindruck entstehen, so ist dies unsererseits auf keinen Fall gewollt oder beabsichtigt. Die in diesem Magazin enthaltenen Angaben wurden nach bestem Wissen erstellt. Trotzdem sind inhaltliche und sachliche Fehler nicht vollständig auszuschließen. Deshalb erfolgen alle Angaben ohne Garantie des Verlags und der Autoren. Für die Inhalte übernehmen wir keinerlei Gewähr oder Verantwortung.   COPYRIGHT: All rights reserved. No part of this work may be reproduced or used in any form or by any means - without written permission from the author and the publisher. Any mentioned person and/ or actions are fictitious. Should there be any similarity to a real existing person or an action, or should such an impression could be originated, it has not been the intention by any means. All information published in this magazine have been produced to the best of one's knowledge. Nevertheless, mistakes regarding contents and objectivity cannot be eliminated completely. Therefore, all the specifications can only be published without guarantee from the publisher's and the author's side. For the contents, there will be no warranty or guarantee.

Taycan 4 Cross Turismo
Stromverbrauch kombiniert in kWh/100 km: 28,1 (NEFZ); 26,4–22,4 (WLTP);
CO_2-Emissionen kombiniert in g/km: 0 (NEFZ); 0 (WLTP);
elektrische Reichweite in km: 389-456 (WLTP) · 463-541 (WLTP innerorts); Stand 08/2021

Electricity consumption combined in kWh/100km: 28,1 (NEDC); 26,4-22,4 (WLTP);
CO_2 emissions combined in g/km: 0 (NEDC); 0 (WLTP);
Range combined in km: 389-456 · Range City in km: 463-541 (WLTP)

IMPRESSUM / IMPRINT

HERAUSGEBER/
PUBLISHER: CURVES MAGAZIN
THIERSCHSTRASSE 25
D-80538 MÜNCHEN

VERANTWORTLICH FÜR
DEN HERAUSGEBER/
RESPONSIBLE FOR
PUBLICATION:
STEFAN BOGNER

KONZEPT/CONCEPT:
STEFAN BOGNER
THIERSCHSTRASSE 25
D-80538 MÜNCHEN
SB@CURVES-MAGAZIN.COM

DELIUS KLASING
CORPORATE PUBLISHING
SIEKERWALL 21
D-33602 BIELEFELD

REDAKTION/
EDITORIAL CONTENT:
STEFAN BOGNER
BEN WINTER

ART DIRECTION, LAYOUT,
FOTOS/ART DIRECTION,
LAYOUT, PHOTOS:
STEFAN BOGNER

MAKING OF FOTOS:
MICHAEL DAIMINGER

TEXT/TEXT: BEN WINTER
TEXT INTRO/TEXT INTRO:
BEN WINTER

MOTIVAUSARBEITUNG
LITHOGRAPHIE/SATZ/
POST-PRODUCTION,

LITHOGRAPHY/SETTING:
MICHAEL DORN

KARTENMATERIAL/MAP
MATERIAL: MAIRDUMONT,
OSTFILDERN

ÜBERSETZUNG/TRANSLATION
JAMES O'NEILL

PRODUKTIONSLEITUNG/
PRODUCTION MANAGEMENT:
AXEL GERBER

DRUCK/PRINT:
KUNST- UND WERBEDRUCK
BAD OEYNHAUSEN

1. AUFLAGE/1ST EDITION:
ISBN: 978-3-667-12285-8

AUSGEZEICHNET MIT / AWARDED WITH
DDC GOLD - DEUTSCHER DESIGNER CLUB E.V. FÜR GUTE GESTALTUNG // IF COMMUNICATION DESIGN AWARD 2012
BEST OF CORPORATE PUBLISHING // ADC BRONZE // RED DOT BEST OF THE BEST & D&AD // NOMINIERT FÜR
DEN DEUTSCHEN DESIGNPREIS 2015 // WINNER AUTOMOTIVE BRAND CONTEST 2014 // GOOD DESIGN AWARD 2014

CURVES AUSGABEN / OTHER ISSUES OF CURVES

PYRENÄEN
PYRENEES
Im Handel erhältlich/Available in stores

ÖSTERREICH
AUSTRIA
Im Handel erhältlich/Available in stores

SCHWEIZ
SWITZERLAND
Im Handel erhältlich/Available in stores

SCHOTTLAND
SCOTLAND
Im Handel erhältlich/Available in stores

FRANKREICH
FRANCE
Im Handel erhältlich/Available in stores

USA · KALIFORNIEN
USA · CALIFORNIA
Im Handel erhältlich/Available in stores

SIZILIEN
SICILY
Im Handel erhältlich/Available in stores

NORDITALIEN
NORTHERN ITALY
Im Handel erhältlich/Available in stores

DEUTSCHLAND/DÄNE.
GERMANY/DENMARK
Im Handel erhältlich/Available in stores

SPANIEN · MALLORCA
SPAIN · MALLORCA
Im Handel erhältlich/Available in stores

USA · COLORADO/UTAH
USA · COLORADO/UTAH
Im Handel erhältlich/Available in stores

THAILAND
THAILAND
Im Handel erhältlich/Available in stores

SÜDDEUTSCHLAND
SOUTHERN GERMANY
Im Handel erhältlich/Available in stores

PORTUGAL
PORTUGAL
Im Handel erhältlich/Available in stores

Soulfood für den Abenteuerhunger.

Der Taycan Cross Turismo. Soul, electrified.

Stromverbrauch kombiniert in kWh/100 km: 29,4 (NEFZ); 26,4–24,4 (WLTP); CO_2-Emissionen kombiniert in g/km: 0 (NEFZ); 0 (WLTP); elektrische Reichweite in km: 388–419 (WLTP) · 460–495 (WLTP innerorts); Stand 07/2021